This book is dedicated to my husband Craig and my daughter Evie for their unconditional love and support. For my true inspirational friend Andrea Rowe who sadly is no longer with us.

An introduction to
The Gateway Journey Workshops, Retreats
and Study Programmes

Contents

Introduction

My name is Gail Donnan and I have had the privilege to work in the well-being industry for the last twenty-five years. I have helped many people to understand anxiety, find or re-claim their personal power, recover from burn out, manage stress and improve their well-being. This book brings together some of the wisdom I have gained as a mindfulness practitioner, meditation teacher, reiki master teacher practitioner, coach, qi gong instructor, holistic therapist, counsellor and teacher.

I write from two perspectives - one is from living through anxiety, stress, depression and burn out and the other is as a qualified well-being practitioner. I have encountered several life challenges including post-traumatic stress, divorce, the death of a close friend, burn out, anxiety, panic, fatigue, depression and have mastered these using different techniques so that I continue to have a successful and happy life.

Over the years I have learnt how to build resilience using mindfulness, meditation, self-development, gathering wisdom, learning about vibrational energy and self-mastery. I now have the pleasure of owning The Mindfulspace Wellbeing Company based in Ripon, North Yorkshire, UK, which is an accredited training centre incorporating two well-being studios and consulting rooms.

With hindsight, I regard the challenges I went through, and continually go through, as tremendous gifts. My wish for anyone reading and using this book is to inspire them to embark on a journey of self-mastery and empowerment and then to repay it by passing on the techniques and benefits to others in need. This book is not a magic bullet; self-development is where the real magic happens.

It takes real courage to look at your life and to make a change. It is far too easy to busy yourself with distractions which can often worsen the situation. Over the years, I have helped and supported many clients and students on a one to one basis. Some of them have been kind enough to share their experiences in this book for which I am eternally grateful. Reading other people's stories and connecting with them can be the beacon of hope and the vehicle for inspiration and change. Also included are some of the most inspirational quotes, from people I admire, that have been important to me. This book is an introduction to my work and offers a starting point for you to move forward.

When you wish to continue your quest, come and join me on a Gateway Journey workshop or retreat in order to further study The Gateway Journey programme at your own pace and in your own time.

More information can be found online at www.gaildonnan.com

A good friend tagged me into this anonymous quote, *"If you hang out with me for too long, I will brainwash you into believing in yourself and knowing that you can achieve anything."* This made me laugh and I was very flattered. Joking aside, this book gives you permission to explore your body and brain, the effects and causes of stress and work on your own self-development, in order to understand yourself better.
I hope you enjoy the journey.

Chapter 1
My Healing Journey

My personal healing journey began after experiencing mental health issues which I saw, at the time, as a sense of failure rather than as being essential to my personal development and change. Prior to the birth of my daughter in 2005, I was the National Sales Manager for a prestigious skin care brand in the UK managing a large team of people. I worked long hours, travelled a lot and had the pleasure of working with some of the best spas, clinics and salons in the UK, Eire and the Channel Islands.

I left my job to take a career break in order to bring up my daughter. Following complications during the birth Evie was born with cranial problems, which we were unaware of at the time. She had problems feeding, lying flat, sleeping and also developed chronic eczema. Lack of sleep, worry and the feeling of not being able to protect her took its toll on me. Life had changed so much from the one I had left behind and I developed what the doctor thought was post-natal depression. It was during this time that I started taking anti-depressants and embarked on some counselling. My daughter was also treated by a cranial osteopath and after the first treatment she fell asleep on her own. For me, this was a turning point with the start of normal life and sleep resuming.

After talking to mums at local groups, it was clear that others were struggling with similar issues but were scared to speak about it. I then decided to train as a counsellor, not only to help me work all this out, but also to be in a position to help other struggling mums find a voice. I realised that, for me, there was a pattern emerging – because I didn't have the perfect baby and life was not as I had expected, I made myself feel quite unhappy. This pattern has continued in my life. Now, using mindfulness, I am able to observe that my mood and temper change when things are not going as expected and I try to remember that it is ok to have a melt-down, I just don't need to unpack my things and live there permanently because it will pass.

After my training, and from speaking to trained colleagues over the years, I now know I suffered from Post-Traumatic Stress Disorder (PTSD) arising from the birth and ensuing complications with my baby rather than post-natal depression.

Looking back, despite what life dealt me, I seemed to cope by simply existing rather than living. It was the death of a very close friend in 2011 that caused a level of trauma, anxiety and panic so huge that at times I retreated to my bed. My whole world was turned upside down, I began questioning my own mortality and the precious gift that is life. I became very scared as I thought my anxiety was never going to go away.

My symptoms came in the form of palpitations, sweating, nervous twitches, teeth clenching, feeling sick, tightness in the chest, a tingling feeling at the base of my neck, churning stomach, absolute fear or dread on waking (similar to waking from a nightmare or bad dream), fatigue, upset tummy, pins and needles in my arms and legs, tears, insomnia, shaking. At times it felt like I was looking down on myself, my peripheral vision became blurred, I couldn't concentrate and grew forgetful. I became good at acting out my own life in order to keep things together; everything was an effort, I had dark thoughts and couldn't find joy in anything. Eventually, in 2014 after a particularly bad day I was taken to hospital in an ambulance. Following an ECG scan, a very kind Doctor asked me if anything was worrying me. I simply said, "How long have you got?"

During the PTSD period, my GP had prescribed me anti-depressants which seemed to work. This time anti-depressants weren't the right approach as they just made me worse. I was frustrated because I had worked in the well-being industry, I was a trained holistic therapist and knew I should be able to fix what was wrong with me. One lonely, dark day I decided to re-visit my reiki roots and use meditation again.

Meditation gave me some space away from my churning thoughts, allowing me to sleep for the first time in months and it started to connect me to my intuition. This was extremely empowering in my own healing because as my brain relaxed through meditation I started to be 'given' little snippets of information indicating that my self-esteem was in tatters. Meditation became quite addictive and that was when a lot of the internal work began for me.

This led me to research ego and mindfulness, both of which provided light bulb moments and actually changed my life. I went on to gain qualifications in mindfulness and meditation and began paying these skills forward in the form of local meditation classes and mindfulness workshops. As a teacher, I like passing on information and seeing the joy I gave to others through my work made me realise that I had at last found my purpose.

In 2015 I set up The Mindfulspace Wellbeing Company to encourage the use of mindfulness and meditation by providing workshops and classes. A BBC journalist picked up my story and filmed a piece of my work in schools for a BBC documentary. Having an educational background, my dream was to teach others so that the work could expand and continue.

The centre opened in February 2017 and it has become a hub for like-minded souls, both individuals and professionals. I worked hard creating courses and gaining accreditation with an awarding body.

Within six months the centre had expanded to double its size and we added regular meditation classes, a one to one mindfulness program, counselling, a treatment menu, workshops galore, yoga, Pilates, sound therapies, baby massage, Qi gong, retreats and self-development book clubs. Today I teach qualifications in mindfulness, meditation, massage, Indian head massage, reiki, baby massage and yoga instructor, holistic facials and deep tissue massage.

The centre also supports local charities, I speak about mental health issues and take my work out into the wider community.

Come and visit us at: www.mindfulspacemeditation.org

"Don't forget you're human.
It's ok to have a meltdown,
just don't unpack and live
there. Cry it out and then
refocus on where you are
headed"

Unknown

Chapter 2
The Gateway Journey

Over the last twenty-five years I have studied many healing systems from Japan, India and China which I use and practise today. The body of this book results from courses, programs and workshops that I have written and delivered over the years. These Eastern cultures work from a view that the mind and body is seen as interconnected and is treated as a whole - holistically. Eastern medicine, or healing, is designed to prevent and treat sickness whereas western medicine only treats sickness when and where it arises. We tend to 'learn' Western healing and 'live' Eastern healing. Every technique in this book is something I have tried that has worked for me and when passed on to my clients has also succeeded for them. I trust that they will work for you too.

I first designed The Gateway Journey as a program for clients who visited me for hourly sessions. The program really gets results and has helped many people find their personal power and purpose. I now want to share the wisdom from The Gateway Journey with you in the form of this book. The system I have designed leads to recovery. This book offers a modified version of the process.

Recovery from low mood, anxiety, panic, fatigue and depression using The Gateway Journey starts with building a bank of personal resilience. This is achieved through understanding anxiety and the reactions of the body and the brain while discovering the benefits of learning how to meditate, together with mindfulness techniques and other helpful ideas to empower change.

The only constant in life is change – we have to accept that suffering exists and what counts is equipping ourselves to get through it in the best possible way. What separates happy and unhappy people is how they interpret and process life's circumstances. From a young age in the West we are taught the opposite of mindfulness. We are constantly wanting, always looking and working towards the next thing, wishing it was the weekend, counting down the days to our holiday, working to buy stuff we don't really need and working to live. We are impressed by material gain rather than living our purpose.

The issues we face today are not new; what has changed significantly is the world in which we live and the speed at which we live our lives. These bring anxieties and stress that can manifest themselves as fatigue and depression. Most of my clients find their way to me because some part of their lives has become disrupted and out of balance. Once investigated the underlying reason is most often due to one of the common issues covered in the next section.

"Knowing yourself is the beginning of all wisdom"

Aristotle

PART ONE: ISSUES

Chapter 3
Stress

Stress is a reaction to the abnormal demands of everyday life. It is a healthy, natural, hormonal reaction that helps us to tackle challenging situations.

In response to a demand, the body reacts first by releasing the catecholamine hormones, adrenaline and norepinephrine, giving the body extra energy and alertness and then the glucocorticoid hormones, cortisol and cortisone which allow a fight, flight or freeze response. These are reactions which have helped the human race to survive since pre-historic times.

Life today is very different to how it was only a few years ago. We have become very competitive and time pressured. It is almost a badge of honour to be busy. Technology is constantly changing, offering more distractions, more comparison and a fear of missing out. Unfortunately, marriage/partnership breakdowns are common and long-term job security seems to be something of the past. It is hardly surprising that at times we feel we simply cannot cope.

In order to enjoy life, we need healthy challenges that we feel we can handle, it is all about balance. But sadly, there are times when we face demands that we feel unable to manage and it is then that we experience stress.

Effects of stress

A certain amount of stress is good for us. It gives us the motivation to achieve our tasks or goals. At these times adrenaline and other chemicals released into our system help us to focus. Stress is the wear and tear we experience as we adjust to our continually changing environment, and it can create both positive and negative physical or emotional effects. When it has a positive influence, it can compel us into action, resulting in a new awareness and an exciting fresh outlook. However, the negative influence can bring feelings of anger, rejection and depression which can lead to health problems, such as headaches, upset stomachs, insomnia, ulcers, high blood pressure, heart disease and stroke.

Recognising the stress response

There are three responses to stress: fight, flight and freezing.
When we are faced with a situation that our bodies interpret as a demand being made upon it, the following reactions occur:

Fight and Flight

- Adrenaline is released, the senses are activated and we become mentally alert
- Our breathing rate speeds up, our nostrils and air passages in our lungs open wider in order to get more air in quickly
- Our heartbeat speeds up and our blood pressure rises
- Sweating increases to help cool the body
- Blood and nutrients are concentrated in the muscles to provide extra strength

Freeze

If the threat is so overwhelming that we have neither the ability to defend ourselves or the strength to run away, our bodies freeze, or dissociate, as the only and possibly best thing it can do in this life-threatening situation and generate:

- Endorphins - an analgesic to reduce the pain of injury to your body or psyche
- Paralysis - a loss of muscle function making it impossible to move

Various anxiety states including phobias, panic attacks and compulsive behaviours often have their origins in a freeze response, probably suffered as a child, that has never fully thawed out resulting in a continuing feeling of distress or post-traumatic stress disorder.

It is rare that events present a physical danger nowadays, but they can still be sufficient enough to produce the fight or flight reaction. Freeze reactions are more common in children who have lower physical resources to cope with real or perceived danger. However, if all the pent-up energy provided by adrenaline is not put to use, the physical results of the stress response will continue, with the body remaining on full alert for long periods of time. It is this long-term response which adversely affects our physical and mental well-being.

The ability to tolerate stress is linked to our individual personalities, our relationships, our resilience and energy levels, together with our emotional maturity. Consequently, introverted people are generally more comfortable with less stimulus than more extroverted individuals.

There are many causes of stress, the three major ones are covered below.

Major Life Changes

Often stress can arise through change, uncertainty and lack of control. Major life changes are the greatest contributor of stress for most of us because they place the greatest demand on our resources for coping. Our lives are a series of constant change. Moving house, entering college, transferring to a new school, getting married, becoming pregnant, starting a new job, losing a job, getting divorced or the death of a loved one are all well-known stress factors. Unhappy relationships tend to be draining and lower our resistance to stress.

Environmental Events

Other stressors can occur through environmental events such as fear of missing out, the pressure from social media, our tendency to engage with competition and comparison, disappointments, time pressures, money problems, noise pollution, illness and caring for dependants.

Work Related Stress

Many people suffer from stress at work which can range from, excessive workload, unrealistic deadlines, insufficient workload, lack of control, poor support, insufficient training, promotion, bullying or harassment, a blame culture, ineffective management, reporting to multiple line managers, an uncertain work future and a poor physical working environment.

Possible Sources of Stress Exercise

When energy levels are reduced, our mechanisms for dealing with the world around us are less robust. Therefore it is important that we learn how to identify and deal with our sources of stress and take positive action whenever we encounter a stressful situation in order to reduce the risk of it seriously impairing our long-term mental and physical health.

- Have you had any major life changes in the last twelve months?
- Have you had any environmental changes in the last twelve months?
- Are you experiencing stress at work or at home?
- Are your issues long or short term?

Manage Stress by Recognising what you can Change

- Can you shorten your exposure to stress?
- Is there anyone you can talk to about what is troubling you?
- Can you reduce the intensity of stress?
- Can you devote the time and energy to making a change?
- Are you viewing your stressors in exaggerated terms and/or taking a difficult situation and catastrophizing it?
- Are you expecting to please everyone?
- Are you overthinking situations?

Actions to Alleviate Stress

- Use deep breathing techniques to moderate your physical reaction to stress
- Build your physical reserves through cardiovascular exercise (walking, jogging, cycling or swimming)
- Eat well-balanced, nutritious meals
- Avoid nicotine, excessive caffeine and other stimulants
- Take breaks
- Put an automatic reply on your emails
- Get enough sleep
- Connect with friends
- Relax with the Five Minute Meditation at www.gaildonnan.com/meditations

Tim's Story

I was the first born in our family and during my early and pre-school years was wrapped in cotton wool due to being an ill baby. I hated school, and now assume I had attachment issues so I built my confidence around sport.

Sadly, I was sexually assaulted as a young teen by an adult family friend and I didn't understand the severity of this until I was older and wiser. I went on to set up an incredibly successful business that is still going from strength to strength twenty years later. I work bloody hard, giving 110% to everything which is not humanly possible and realised this can contribute to stress and your downfall.

On my honeymoon I survived an airplane crash and assisted the majority of the passengers from the sea into a boat which left a huge impact on me. During the early years of marriage, I was told I couldn't have children, it broke my heart having to tell my wife the news. She was put on this planet to reproduce and I could not provide. I later found out that two hernia operations as a child had damaged my sperm ducts and, on an ultrasound, it looked like I'd had a vasectomy. On hindsight I realised I had started to develop anger issues.

After five emotionally painful and expensive IVF treatments we finally had three children; first a beautiful girl and then the devil twin boys! The journey was truly a roller coaster ride but they have brought me utter love and happiness but my demons from my past still existed in my head.

As a father my past came to haunt me because my anxieties went crazy and I became extremely over protective. The assault in my teens became fresh in my mind as the offender was sent to prison for numerous child offences. The realisation that I was not on my own gave me hope, but I became so angry, I had not told anyone for a decade, except my wife, but am now in my late thirties and realised I needed to deal with it.

I did not want my past to affect my future life and I wanted to be the best dad I could be, I did not want to have a mid-life crisis or fall apart. I needed to be strong, protective and the earner in the household.

I decided I needed to talk to someone and get some help which led me to mindfulness therapy. I met with Gail and I instantly felt at home. I think we were destined to meet because it all fell into place and I was able to address my issues. I had not realised how angry I had become internally and it felt great letting that go.

I was worried about everything and mostly things utterly out of my control. Breathing techniques helped but it was a change in my thought process and the realisation that I cannot sustain being superman however much I tried.

After mindfulness therapy I am living my life for the now. I am spending time with my family and not trying to keep up with anybody else. It is my life, everyone has bad times but it is how we learn to deal with them. I have been blown away by mindfulness and intend to learn more and train to become a coach myself in the future. Gail is an inspiration and a life saver.

"My mission in life is
not merely to survive, but
to thrive; and to do it
with some passion, some
compassion, some humour
and some style"

Maya Angelou

Chapter 4
Depression

We all have basic emotional needs that must be met in order for us to thrive, survive and enjoy our lives. After the primary human need for food, water and shelter, come our commonly shared emotional and physical needs. Depression arises when one or more of these basic needs are not being met.

The term depression is commonly used to describe the unhappiness or distress that follows an unpleasant event. This type of depression is a completely normal response, is short-lived, and is usually resolved pretty quickly without the need for therapy or treatment. In contrast, depressive illness is a much more severe condition, affecting the way you feel, think and act. Constant feelings of sadness together with negativity cause difficulties in coping and an inability to find joy in anything. Sadly, depression will affect one in four of us at some stage of our lives.

Those who have not suffered from depression find it hard to understand and think the person can just snap out of it. To try to explain depression would be to recall the most distressed state you have ever experienced and imagine that feeling continuing for months for no obvious reason.

Causes

Separation, divorce, serious illness, a family history of depression as well as chronic medical conditions or a major life change can all increase the risk of developing depression.

Depression has a chemical and biological basis and many researchers believe it is caused by an imbalance of two naturally-occurring chemicals – serotonin and norepinephrine – in the brain and body. In the brain, these chemicals are thought to be associated with mood and the regulation and reduction of physical pain felt in the body. Positive life experiences increase levels of our happy chemical serotonin just as modern anti-depressants do. Negative worry, guilt, regret and over thinking all reduce our serotonin levels.

Once these chemicals are out of balance you can feel the effects in both the brain and the body. Avoiding caffeine, alcohol, drugs and stimulants can therefore be a useful first step to recovery.

Only a qualified doctor or health practitioner can formally diagnose clinical depression. If you can see beyond the sadness it is likely that it is a low mood that will pass, while true depression often makes you feel that things will always be this way. Once these patterns take hold they start to affect you physically. Women experience depression twice as often as men, perhaps because women tend to be more likely to share and seek treatment, although men are much more likely to commit suicide as a result of a depressive illness. Male depression can often be masked by alcohol, drugs or the socially acceptable habit of working excessively. Men are less likely to feel sad or hopeless, instead depression tends to manifest as anger, irritability and discouragement.

Many hormonal factors may contribute to the reason why more women suffer with depression. Hormonal changes during the menstrual cycle, pregnancy, miscarriage and menopause may be factors. Women these days also face additional stress from working full time, being the primary carer of children, single parenthood or caring for elderly parents and young children.

Hormonal changes, difficult birth, lack of sleep and the sheer responsibility for a new life can also lead to postnatal depression.

Seasonal Affective Disorder

Some people are affected by the shorter days and the descent of the dark and gloom of late autumn and the onset of winter. Researchers have found that the production of the feel good neurotransmitter serotonin in the brain is directly related to the amount of time we are exposed to bright sunlight. Consequently seasonal affective disorder (SAD) is a form of depression that tends to come and go with the seasons and is worse during the winter. Getting as much natural sunlight as possible, exercising regularly while alleviating stress can make a big difference to managing this condition.

Stress

Depressive illness can result from a build-up of stress which eventually causes a breakdown in the body's chemistry and triggers depressive episodes. Stress has its own chapter in this book.

Symptoms and Management

Everyone is unique and depression affects each of us in different ways and with differing types of symptoms.

Psychological

These include experiencing a feeling of constant sadness which makes it difficult to enjoy life or feel positive about anything. It gives us a sensation of looking in on yourself and a feeling of being completely overwhelmed with life together with the inability to tolerate uncertainty. These may lead to further intrusive and upsetting thoughts so that we can't see a way out of our situation. We may become extremely anxious and exhausted with all this procrastinating.

Relaxation techniques including meditation and deep breathing can offer relief.

Listen to the ten minute Releasing Negative Thoughts Meditation at
www.gaildonnan.com/meditations

Physical

Depression affects our physical body and can disrupt our sleep patterns with insomnia and early wakening that leave us exhausted, and lacking in enough energy to see us through the day ahead. At this point it is tempting to use energy drinks or caffeine – these can simply overstimulate our nervous system and disrupt our body's chemical balance. Avoiding alcohol, tobacco and stimulants during this time will help to restore our body into balance. Depression can make us tearful and our mood can be low, a simple activity such as a brisk walk can produce enough endorphins and serotonin to lighten our mood.

Social

Depression is often an isolating illness that causes us to withdraw from social occasions and connections because they are too much of an effort. We may feel we are being a burden on our family and friends. It is important to try sharing how you feel with others and sustain social connections because these are the very things essential for recovery. Try a visit to the cinema or theatre, or exercising with a group of friends.

Men and Women

Research suggests that men and women share the same core symptoms of depression but women tend to show more emotional symptoms than men. It is thought that these differences occur because traditional gender roles allow women to communicate their feelings and seek help, while men are expected to be strong and cope. When men do not allow themselves to express their feelings, they may manifest in other forms, such as anger attacks.

Interestingly, men and women's symptoms differ as women are more likely than men to exhibit the atypical symptoms of depression, like sleeping excessively and overeating, in contrast to the typical symptoms, such as insomnia and loss of appetite.

Men show other signs of depression that may differ from women in the form of abusing alcohol or other substances, escaping by staying at work late, risk-taking or recklessness, exploding in anger, becoming controlling, violent or abusive.

Managing Depression

Depression alters our thought patterns so it becomes difficult to think rationally and we may need to reach out for some professional help in the form of talking therapies or medication. Speak to someone if you feel suicidal. Avoid making important decisions until the depression has lifted. It is worth remembering that most people recover from depression but feeling better does take time. Depression is by no means a failure, so give yourself permission to take time out. Set realistic goals for yourself each day, assume a reasonable, but not excessive, amount of responsibility. Think about what activities you can do that you enjoy and which will make you feel better.

Listen to the Releasing Negative Emotions Meditation at
www.gaildonnan.com/meditations

Catherine's Story

In January 2016 my world came crashing down and my life changed in just one day. My husband of only six months left me homeless and penniless. For 18 months I sofa-surfed staying with friends and family. Then depression hit; the emotional and physical trauma that I had sustained in my relationship came to a head. It was too much for me to handle and I went into a self-destructive mode. I drank ridiculous amounts of alcohol just to get through the pain.

The result was a severe breakdown. I felt lost, alone, scared, and humiliated, as well as stupid and naïve. I stopped eating and dropped two stone, I felt as though someone had dug my insides out with a teaspoon. I was empty, had no soul, no voice, no love and no laughter, I felt suicidal and unloved.

One day I cried all day at work, I had never felt so low, I just wanted to go to sleep and to not wake up. I had been having suicidal thoughts for around two weeks and stood on Knaresborough Bridge contemplating throwing myself over.

Around the time of my first wedding anniversary I planned a break to travel to stay with a cousin in America. I didn't enjoy my trip, I could hardly eat and lost even more weight. On my return I decided to start eating properly and on a shopping trip came across a mindfulness book that contained the words by Lao Tzu, "A journey of a thousand miles begins…".

As I read, I began to change my habits one by one, it gave me strength to chase my dreams, to lose the fear and gave me back my life. I started to read inspirational quotes and watch personal development videos. I told myself every day "you have got this shit" and I fought every day for my life and my self-worth. I started listening to meditation music to help me sleep.

One day I spoke to a friend who had gone travelling and realised that I didn't want to waste anymore of my life, so I booked a working holiday to Thailand and Australia. After a big 30th birthday party, I headed off on my trip. It was during these travels that I decided to come home and finalise my divorce.

In September 2017, when I was out of work with a broken wrist, I decided a career change was needed. I wanted to share my story in order to support others, so I began a social media campaign and blog. I post positive quotes, affirmations, meditations and mindfulness walking ideas. This spurred a lot of messages from people saying how brave I had been and how inspirational I was. For me it was a choice of living, not giving up and not letting another person destroy me because I am worth so much more.

I decided to study mindfulness and meditation and I have set up my own meditation classes. I also sell meditation packs and £1 from each pack goes to the mental health charity Mind. I plan to live in Australia and have my own retreat centre offering mindfulness, meditation and holistic therapies.

A journey of a thousand miles does begin with just one step, and my beautiful wise friend Sadie also gave me the best encouragement which was, "If you don't jump you will always stay in the same spot." Mindfulness has helped my recovery and taught me to love myself and others because the world needs more love.

"Holding onto anger is like drinking poison and expecting the other person to die"

Anon

Chapter 5
Anxiety

We all experience anxiety, that feeling of worry, nervousness or apprehension, in situations where we feel insecure, unsure or afraid. It has been estimated that up to 5% of the population has, at some time, experienced anxiety to such an extent that it can be classified as an anxiety disorder and sadly this condition is on the rise. Chronic anxiety can range from feeling uncomfortable to being extremely debilitating, giving rise to symptoms such as panic attacks, phobias, obsessive compulsive thoughts and behaviours or a generalized feeling of anxiety and fear in situations where there is no real cause for concern.

Fortunately, anxiety responds well to listening therapies, meditation and relaxation techniques which offer a sense of control. As most anxiety disorders are psychological in origin, symptoms may sometimes accompany medical problems such as hyperthyroidism, nutritional deficiencies, chemical and hormonal imbalances, headaches and tension.

My response to anxiety has been to learn about it. This understanding has empowered me and taken the fear away. The training I have received in counselling, anatomy and physiology have given me great insight into the systems of the body and its chemical dispositions. Our endocrine system, containing all the hormone producing glands, plays a major part in anxiety, and these chemicals flowing through our bodies are extremely powerful.

Why do we get Anxious?

Anxiety is generally fear based and part of our natural survival mechanism. The amygdala in the brain is responsible for responding to fear and instructs the endocrine system to protect us in times of danger or stress with high levels of adrenaline and cortisol producing our fight, flight or freeze responses. We have ancient brains trying to cope in a modern-day world and as we no longer have to face woolly mammoths or sabre tooth tigers, these chemicals flood our bodies creating a high state of stress that leads us to flee situations we find threatening, lash out or do things we later regret.

Anxiety has therefore become a modern illness. Today we have so much to do, dashing from one place to the other, answering emails, checking social media, working against the clock, which results in the amygdala constantly turning on our stress response. We often feel fearful that we don't have enough time in the day for what we hope to achieve. Because of this we spend long periods of the day fired with adrenaline and cortisol, which is physically exhausting and can cause adrenal problems, heart problems, panic attacks, low mood, anxiety and depression.

On bad days, anxiety can cause us to wake up with a dark, sinking feeling of dread without explanation. It is good to remind ourselves that we are all a work in progress; when you feel your anxiety creeping back, stop, rest, do some deep breathing or try a meditation exercise. The anxiety will pass if you don't feed it with more fear, and celebrate the fact that your body is trying to protect you, by being kind to yourself. When you feel stronger, perhaps examine the internal fears that may be triggering your anxiety. A better understanding of your body and mind bring the realisation that perhaps you are just trying to achieve too much or over thinking, which can tip your chemical balance allowing nervous fatigue to set in.

During the time I was at my lowest with anxiety, a friend suggested a book recommended by a GP to a family member who was going through a tough time. It was, "Essential Help for Your Nerves" (Harper Collins, 2000) written by Dr Claire Weekes, universally acclaimed for her work on nervous illness. Her words literally changed my life.

One of the pleasures that anxiety robbed me of was the ability to read or concentrate. Her book understands this and has been deliberately written in short chapters in order to make it easier to absorb. Not all of the book was relevant to me; however, it did help me understand nervous fatigue, which can manifest as muscular, mental and emotional or when your soul is exhausted, spiritual fatigue. It also explained how it creeps up on you gradually over a long period of time so you don't really notice it. Once I could give what I had a name and recognise it as nervous fatigue, I experienced a degree of relief. Her book played a pivotal part in my healing journey.

One word that stood out to me was 'sensitisation' which Dr Weekes believes is the prime cause of emotional fatigue from an overabundance of adrenaline running through the body. This excess exaggerates all our emotions and gradually depletes our energy, it is a chemical process that has perhaps taken months to creep up and manifest, so we must also allow time for recovery and adjustment.

Another symptom that resonated with me was 'the shock of waking'. At the time when I woke up, I would have strong feelings of foreboding, a racing heart and the sensation of being plugged in at the mains even though my body felt like it wasn't there at all.

The techniques she advocates are:

- Acceptance - do not fight or resist what is happening
- Facing - acknowledge and understand that the cure comes from within you
- Floating - be kind to yourself, slow your life down, achieve what you can and allow time to pass as being impatient only creates more tension

Mindfulness and meditation techniques are closely aligned with the r
she advises for anyone recovering from nervous fatigue.

Finally, she explains recovery comes by trying not to be so upset by the physical symptoms or your exaggerated emotional reactions. Eventually I started to notice small pockets of the day during which I felt normal, these pockets turned into minutes, then minutes into hours. My recovery took six months through understanding my body and my energy better, self-care, self-honouring, mindfulness and meditation.

Self Help

When you are feeling anxious, empower yourself and take back control by giving yourself the gift of time, nothing is so important that it can't wait, therefore learn to rest. The physical symptoms and exaggerated emotions that accompany anxiety can be troubling. Avoid letting them upset you by reminding yourself that your body is simply raising an alarm to a potential threat. Create realistic, achievable goals for your day, ask for help with the chores and stop multi-tasking or attempting to do too much.

Meditation and yoga induce relaxation and calm, allowing thoughts and emotions to pass while helping you live in the now. You will find a breathing exercise in this chapter that will move you into a more relaxed state. Lavender and vetiver are relaxing essential oils that can be used in a diffuser around the home, car or office. Rescue remedy is a Bach Flower remedy which is thought to calm the nervous system and is available in pharmacies in spray, drops and sweet formats. Finally if you feel your anxiety is affecting your day, share how you are feeling with someone you trust or contact your GP for support.

Deep Breathing Exercise

We need to breathe to stay alive. When we encounter stress, our breath shortens which sends a danger alert to the brain. Learning to focus on our breath during stressful times is a powerful technique as deep breathing moves the body into a more relaxed state.

Adjust as required to suit your breathing abilities

- Stop and sit down
- Turn all notifications on your phone off
- Set a timer/alarm for 10 minutes
- Close your eyes, shut out the sounds and focus on your breathing
- For the first couple of minutes just notice how you are breathing without making a judgment on it
- Start by breathing in to a slow count of 4 (seconds) and out to a slow count of 4
- After a while, continue breathing in to a slow count of 4, then hold the breath, or do nothing, for 4 seconds and breathe out to a slow count of 4
- After a while continue breathing in to the count of 4, hold for 4 then start breathing out for 6 seconds

David's Story

My journey into self-improvement started well over two years ago. I decided to stop smoking, lose weight and get fit on the fear of not seeing my children get married and have their own children.

Eighteen months into that journey, I lost my father suddenly and found myself battling with anxieties and regrets; and at the time I couldn't see or believe this.

My head was full and my heart was broken. I was living in the past.

A friend pointed me towards Gail and over the next few months, I started to leave some of the past behind and start living in the now. She helped me understand which of my thoughts were imaginary and which are real and how to notice and handle negative thoughts.

I will be forever grateful.

"Nothing ever goes away
until it has taught us
what we need to know"

Pema Chodron

Chapter 6
Pre-menstrual Syndrome (PMS)

Pre-menstrual Syndrome (PMS), (also called pre-menstrual tension (PMT) or pre-menstrual dysphoric depression (PMDD) is a combination of physical and psychological symptoms that occur in some women approximately the week before menstruation begins. It is caused by a variety of factors which differ from person to person. Women who have difficulties with body image or problems surrounding womanhood tend to be more prone to PMS. The biological and physical effects include water retention, fluctuating hormonal levels and a deficiency in serotonin, the feel-good brain chemical.

In my twenties, I was diagnosed with PCOS (Polycystic Ovary Syndrome) which is a hormonal and endocrine disorder. It comes with many ailments but it is closely linked to PMT and depression, and my fluctuating hormone levels make me feel very overwhelmed during the run up to the menstrual cycle. To combat this, I spend more time doing things for me, meditating, running and being kind to myself. I also put off making any important decisions during this time as I understand that my judgement may be skewed and that any irrational thoughts will pass so that normal service can be resumed! During these times keeping a journal helps to identify patterns in the symptoms, which makes them less of a concern and reduces my anxiety levels.

Symptoms of Pre-menstrual Syndrome

Physical symptoms include a change in appetite, craving for sweets and chocolate type foods. It is common to have headaches, stomach complaints, and swollen lymph nodes under the arms, tender breasts, water retention, pelvic pain, backache and increased perspiration. Energy levels can be intensely high followed by fatigue.

PMS also brings psychological, emotional and behavioural symptoms that include irritability, mood swings, and difficulties with impulse control, tearfulness, anxiety, depression and fatigue. Some women experience symptoms which are so debilitating that their day to day functioning and relationships are significantly affected.

Help

Any kind of heat helps. This can be in the form of a hot water bottle, warm wheat bag or heat patch which will relax the muscles of the uterus, increasing blood flow and easing pain and cramping. If you are encountering severe pain seek over the counter pain relief from your pharmacist. Keep well hydrated by drinking plenty of water and herbal tea. Eat nourishing foods to give yourself extra energy. Remind yourself the emotional feelings are transient and will pass. Use a journal to monitor your moods and try distracting yourself by meeting a friend or going for a walk. Balancing essential oils such as geranium and rose can be very restorative and don't forget to get plenty of rest.

"The primary cause of unhappiness is never the situation but your thoughts about it"

Eckhart Tolle

Chapter 7
Fatigue and Sleep

Fatigue is a limiting and overwhelming feeling of exhaustion, both mental and physical, that is not relieved by rest or sleep.

Over the years, I have experienced fatigue caused by anxiety and depression. In my early forties I began to experience panic attacks due to my nervous system having become overloaded with adrenalin and cortisol causing my body to become exhausted and out of balance. The main causes for me were hormonal imbalance, lack of or poor-quality sleep, anxiety, depression and grief.

Reducing Fatigue with Minerals

Bathing in salt water is a good way to reduce fatigue. Our skin is an organ with many functions, one is elimination and the salt will draw toxins and heavy metals from our tissues. In addition, the salt relieves muscular aches and pains while increasing circulation allowing us to bring fresh oxygen, nutrients and essential trace minerals into our bodies.

If you are feeling weighed down, lethargic, negative, under the weather, stressed or over tired, a salt bath can help. Use unprocessed mineral salts such as Himalayan or a natural sea salt like Celtic. If all else fails, ordinary table salt will also do the job as it contains a high amount of sodium although with fewer trace minerals.

Magnesium is an often-overlooked mineral. Known as nature's tranquiliser it is an excellent remedy for fatigue, PMS, headaches, muscle cramps, stress and sleep. A high percentage of us are magnesium deficient and although magnesium is included in most multi vitamins, an extra dose can make a huge difference to our overall well-being.

One downside is that oral magnesium supplements can often cause upset stomachs. Therefore, a good alternative is to absorb it through the skin by relaxing for twenty minutes in a warm bath containing Epsom salts. Once dissolved in water, Epsom salt breaks down into its constituent parts – magnesium and sulphate, and a good soak in its water will help with lack of energy, stress, anxiety and aid relaxation. There are also other ways to take in magnesium, by using oil sprays or booking in for a flotation therapy session, which is a favourite of mine.

Placing small bowls of rock salt around your house help to cleanse the air by drawing out airborne toxins. Alternatively, use a Himalayan salt lamp – a large block of chiselled natural salt with a bulb inside. Because salt is very attractive to water vapour, which carries particles from the air containing allergens like dust, pollen, pet dander, smoke particles, bacteria and viruses, it becomes saturated. As the heat from the salt lamp dries out the water vapour is released back into the air trapping the contaminants in the salt.

Salt lamps are best placed where you spend the most time. The health benefits reported include, improved breathing problems, less colds and flu, increased relaxation, fewer headaches, reduced symptoms from disorders like rheumatism and arthritis, better sleep patterns and a general sense of well-being.

Sleep

Sleep is my go-to healer. Servicing the body on a molecular level both mentally and physically, sleep affects our energy balance, as well as intellectual function, alertness and mood and is crucial to our well-being.

While we sleep, our bodies don't shut down; our brains, internal organs and other processes are hard at work throughout the night affecting growth and stress hormones, our immune system, appetite, breathing, blood pressure and cardiovascular health.

Although our brains work automatically, it is our own innate ability to regulate them that determines how well we cope with pressure, rational and irrational thoughts, work through our tasks and so much more. If our environment and lifestyle cause an overuse or underuse of a certain brain function it can produce many negative effects such as insomnia, anger, stress, learning difficulties or anxiety. Every brain function serves a purpose to help us cope with a variety of situations.

We have five brainwave states, in order of lowest to highest frequency, they are; delta, theta, alpha, beta and gamma. In order for the body to relax and sleep it has to travel through several different brainwave states to get from the highly alert beta stage to the deep, healing sleep of delta. Our brainwave state is a major factor in allowing us to switch off and go to sleep, which can be difficult for some people.

Each frequency, outlined below from lowest to highest, has its own set of characteristics representing a specific level of brain activity.

Delta is our slowest wave. It is experienced in deep, dreamless sleep and in deep meditation where our awareness is separated and is in the domain of our unconscious mind. Deep restorative sleep is important for regeneration and healing. Lower delta waves are produced during the ageing process and they also help regulate the cardiovascular and the digestive systems.

Theta is our light meditation and sleep brainwave state and includes our REM dream state. It is experienced, for a brief period, whilst dropping off to sleep and waking from deep sleep. Theta helps to improve our creativity, inspiration, intuition and is where we experience vivid visualisations. Too much theta activity can cause people to be prone to depression while too little creates anxiety, poor emotional awareness and higher stress levels.

Alpha is our deep relaxation state, the bridge between our conscious thinking and subconscious mind. Alpha waves help calm you down and promote feelings of deeper relaxation and contentment. Low levels of alpha waves can cause obsessive-compulsive disorders (OCD), anxiety and higher stress levels whilst high levels create an over-relaxed state and the inability to concentrate.

Beta brainwaves are associated with normal waking consciousness and acting in an alert, logical and critical state and help our effective functioning during the day but can also turn into stress, anxiety and restlessness. Beta waves cause that nagging little inner critic that gets louder when there is a high state of stress which can become overwhelmed during strenuous periods in life. Beta waves increase when taking caffeine or other stimulants.

Gamma is the most recently discovered brainwave, so our understanding of how it works is still evolving. Research indicates that gamma waves are associated with bursts of insight and high-level information processing and are used to process more complex tasks and also healthy cognitive functions. Researchers are also finding strong links between meditation and gamma waves as the heightened state of being or completeness is experienced when in a meditative state.

Improving Sleep

We have an internal clock that runs in the background of our brain, controlled by part of our hypothalamus, and cycles at regular intervals between sleepiness and alertness creating our natural circadian (daily) rhythm.

Most adults have their biggest dip in energy between 2.00-4.00 am and 1.00-3.00 pm. Outside factors like lightness and darkness also impact, so when it is dark at night, our eyes send a signal to the brain that it is time to feel tired, which in turn sends a signal to your body to release the hormone melatonin which makes you feel sleepy.

Therefore, boosting your melatonin level is beneficial for improving sleep. Foods which maximise melatonin naturally are bananas, morello cherries, oats, rice, ginger, tomatoes, red wine, sweetcorn and radishes. Tryptophan is an essential amino acid that converts into serotonin, melatonin and vitamin B6. Found in milk, soy, nuts, seafood, turkey, chicken, sesame and sunflower seeds, whole grains, rice and eggs, which when combined with a carbohydrate significantly increase the production of melatonin. This is why we often get that sleepy feeling after a large roast dinner, especially if it contains turkey or chicken.

Avoiding potential stimulants such as alcohol, nicotine and caffeine before bed, going to bed and getting up at the same time and taking daily exercise all help to build good sleep habits. Inhaling relaxing, base note essential oils from a bath or diffuser draws the oil molecules into your system and calms the body. Some of my favourites are lavender, vetiver, roman chamomile, ylang ylang, bergamot and sandalwood. Drink herbal night-time tea about an hour before bed; valerian is widely used for improving sleep.

Avoid using bright lights and screens before bed because the light emitted from phones, tablets and laptops trick the brain into thinking it is daylight and will slow down the production of melatonin needed for sleep. For this reason, it is important to set boundaries around screen time prior to bed, particularly for children.

During my mid-forties I began waking up between 1.00-3.00am and had trouble getting back off to sleep. According to traditional Chinese medicine insomnia and poor sleep quality are due to a disturbance in the mind and spirit and waking at this time of the night is down to an imbalance in the liver.

Turmeric curcumin in addition to its anti-inflammatory and anti-oxidant properties is widely used as a natural remedy to promote sleep. Emerging research suggests that a better night's sleep can be gained from using turmeric because of the detoxifying and cleansing effect it has on the liver as it assists a natural enzyme that flushes out dietary carcinogens.

I began making a turmeric latte with coconut or almond milk before bed but found I needed to get up to go to the bathroom during the night, so I changed to using an oral turmeric spray.

This allows the turmeric to be absorbed straight into the blood stream from the soft tissue of the mouth, bypassing the digestive system. I use two sprays in the mornings and two sprays before bed. Now, I rarely wake up during the night and if I do, I never struggle to get back to sleep.

Good Sleep Checklist

- No caffeine after 3 pm
- Eat your evening meal early with melatonin and tryptophan boosting foods
- Limit screen time an hour before bed
- Go to bed and rise at the same time every day
- Enjoy a valerian tea
- Use base note aromatherapy oils in bath, diffuser or pillow spray
- Try a turmeric spray
- Before bed use the Meditation to Induce Sleep at www.gaildonnan.com/meditations

"Quiet the mind
and the soul will speak"

Ma Jaya Sati Bhagavati

Chapter 8
Time

Time is a concept followed by clocks and calendars and it passes by in seconds, minutes, hours, days and years. It is always moving forward but can never move backwards. This is the reason why many of us are fearful of not having enough time, because it is finite, unknown in quantity and we have no choice other than to be carried forward with it.

I meet a lot of people who feel under constant pressure from time, which causes them tremendous anxiety.

Rather than telling the time and watching it slip away, changing our perspective and relationship with time can return a sense of control into our lives and quell some of those anxious feelings. Start by focussing on what time well spent means to you and then create the space for it in your life.

The Timekeeper by Mitch Albom (Hachette, 2015) helped me change my relationship with time. Albom's book is an inspirational fictional story that has made a lasting impression on me. His books are always filled with deep human truth, but this one allowed me to realise how precious, yet how damaging, time can be.

In it, the central character in ancient times invents the first clock and is punished for trying to measure time. Banished for thousands of years becoming Father Time, he has to listen to people moaning about their "lack of time". The poor guy does get the chance to redeem himself when he helps two completely different people with opposite problems to understand the value of time in pretty dramatic circumstances.

Reading this book gave me the opportunity to look at how mindlessly we can live each day and how precious time really is. Whilst reading it, I began to notice time everywhere – my car dashboard, my watch, my alarm clock, our kitchen clock, my phone clock, my diary, the kitchen family calendar and even the clock at work. I perform at my worst when I think I will never get through everything I need to do in the day and it is a horrible, overwhelming feeling, which if I let it, will consume me.

One day I decided to do an experiment and re-plan my day in a different way, which included not wearing a watch, making sure I had a couple of hours free time, turning off my phone, putting my diary away, taking down or turning off the clocks and removing any calendars. After the allotted hours were up, I noticed how calm I had been; I had experienced no anxiety and thoroughly enjoyed the liberation of not being ruled by time.

I then began to wonder how on earth I could experience the same feelings in a normal day of school runs, supermarket shopping, work appointments and meetings. Eventually I figured that I could give myself back some time, by either getting up an hour earlier or scheduling an hour somewhere in the day just for me, so I could spend some time doing exactly what I wanted. After a while this has become habitual and I've settled into this new routine without feelings of guilt. As a result, my anxiety levels have dropped and I am less fearful of time. Albom writes "man alone measures time, man alone chimes the hour. And because of this, man alone suffers a paralysing fear that no other creature endures. A fear of time running out."

Wise words, thank you Mitch.

Change Your Relationship with Time

- Get up earlier and do what takes your fancy, especially easy in the summer
- Schedule some time every day just for you
- Turn your phone off for periods of the day
- Make a "not to do list"

"We have forgotten how to
be good guests, how to walk
lightly on the earth as its
other creatures do"

Barbara Ward

Chapter 9
Technology

Large corporations and advertising companies are helping create a culture of FOMO – the fear of missing out. This in itself creates anxiety. Fast changing technological advances are also having an effect on how we live. We spend so much time scrolling through our addictive smart phones looking at the often unreal and filtered snapshots of other people's lives that we forget to live our own. Smart phones are designed to be addictive in order to collect data through complex algorithms that feed you distractions and lead you into temptation and time wasting. It is no wonder that mental health issues are on the rise and that anxiety is the illness of our time.

We have never lived with so many distractions and so much stimulation and this can be overwhelming. Our brains have changed little from ancient times, yet we live in a fast paced, modern world with its frantic goings-on, expecting not to be engulfed. We are living through a global mental health epidemic, which thankfully it is now ok to talk about. However, there are few solutions and resources available to actually help people.

Like everything in life, we have a choice. We can choose how we use technology. When you feel that scrolling is taking over your day, give yourself back the gift of time and set limits. Don't get me wrong I love my smart phone, I think technology is amazing but only when it serves me. We are apt to forget that technology is here to enable us, not control us.

I have an app on my smart phone which tells me how much time I have spent on it, what I have been doing and how many times I have unlocked my phone during the day. It made me aware that I had a habit of looking at it when I was bored or in need of a distraction. I would find myself picking it up for a diversion or dare I say a "reward" after a chore. Now, I try to be sensible and I have my notifications switched off so I decide when to check email and social media rather than when I hear that seductive "ping".

Technology has given us instant accessibility; the downside is that it also breeds anxiety. I have to constantly tell myself it is ok not to get back to someone until tomorrow or even the next day. I am not a fan of texting and messaging but I understand that for some it works. Personally, I am much happier speaking face to face or over the phone. My husband knows I would rather talk to him during the day instead of texting, which is not always possible, but it is so much nicer to hear his voice.

I am also mindful to be off my phone if possible when I am with my daughter; I want to be present and available to her as much as I can. This not only gives her more of my time and attention, it also provides her with a good role model. Recent studies show a decline in the mental health of young people. One of the contributing factors is that parents are seen as emotionally unavailable to their children due to the instant accessibility culture and relentless demands of technology, coupled with the constant fear of missing out fuelled by social media.

Current research also advocates leaving your phone and computer outside your bedroom or sleeping area because of the impact is has on developing the melatonin you need for sleep.

On the days when I deliberately leave my phone at home or in the car, I feel such a rebel. I really do enjoy a digital detox day; simply making the conscious decision to do without technology allows my head to become clearer and I feel more at peace with myself. These feelings remind me of the days before I got my first mobile phone almost twenty years ago.

Exercise

- Put a regular digital detox day into your diary now
- Download a free app to monitor how often you use your phone
- Have regular set times to check your phone
- Be more discerning about your use of social media
- Switch off all technology an hour before bedtime
- Remove all technology from your sleeping area
- Notice what you do with the extra time not spent using your phone

Nicola's Story

I was a busy working single mum with two teenage children, carrying out extensive renovations to my house, when I became aware that I felt excessively tired. As the long Easter weekend was approaching, I decided that I was going to use the time to recharge, sleep and do very little. After four days I felt no better and returning to work made me feel worse. During this time, I was able to do very little due to extreme fatigue. My body ached as if I had flu. I had fainting attacks. After any short physical activity, I felt weak, light headed and shaky. It felt like I was running on adrenaline all the time. My memory was terrible and I felt unable to make any decision, no matter how simple. Ironically, my sleeping was also disturbed. I could not cope with my job and nobody could give me a definite diagnosis. I did not know when, or if, I would be able to return to my old routine and this just added to my worry.

On a particularly bad day I saw an advert for a mindfulness and meditation workshop and knew that this was what I needed. When Gail explained the role of the amygdala in the stress response and the symptoms of over stimulation, I recognised myself. The relief was huge. These symptoms were not unknown and there were things that I could do to help myself. Suddenly I was certain that I could be well again. I began to include meditation in my daily routine and decided I needed to investigate other mindfulness techniques.

One of the biggest changes for me was when I accepted my situation and stopped trying to fight it. I gave myself permission to take the time I needed to become well. I felt as if a weight had been lifted. I recognised that my body was trying to make me stop the daily treadmill. I knew deep down that I needed to make some changes to my lifestyle and possibly to the way I organised my working life. I knew the changes could be difficult and I had resisted facing them, until now. Instead of finding this frightening, it felt empowering.

I took advantage of the work-free time to meditate and to consider various emotional problems that had occurred in my past. Matters that I had not thought of for years came to the fore, and I was able to take time to deal with these. I have been able to forgive myself for things that have happened and recognise my own self- worth, which has given me an improved confidence.

My energy levels started to improve and I had to be careful not to do too much and deplete the reserves. At times when I did run out of energy a short meditation would help me to recharge and I began to start the day with a meditation rather than scrolling through messages on my phone. Much more positive!

"At any moment you have a choice that either leads you closer to your spirit or further away from it"

Thich Nhat Hanh

PART TWO: SOLUTIONS

Chapter 10
Self Honouring

Self honouring is about taking responsibility for your own happiness.

Not many people understand what the term means – it is all about respecting your own needs and health. Understanding and practising self honouring is where the journey to recovery can often begin.

Authenticity

When you honour yourself, you pay attention to your needs by listening to and acknowledging them. If you start saying no to what feels wrong or consumes your energy and start saying yes to what makes you happy, your body and mind will start to become stronger. When we align ourselves with self-love, self-acceptance and being honest, we become accountable and start to take responsibility for our own happiness. Once we start to be our authentic selves without social conditioning, back story or fear about what others think, we begin to take back our personal power and build resilience.

Recognise Your Needs

If you are someone who gets side-tracked by people pleasing, often confused with kindness, it is time to start letting go of what is no longer serving you. Try not to be influenced by what others define as important, instead pay attention to your own needs. Once you spread yourself too thinly or your default mode becomes that of a people pleaser, then you may end up saying "yes" when you really mean "no". Being too giving generates stress, resentment and anxiety. Once this happens it is time to look at where your energy is leaking. In the past I have been guilty of this as I wanted others to like me; now I realise people will either like me or not regardless of how much I do for them.

Try not to get tied up in the minutiae of what people think, so you can become confident in your own skin and preserve your own personal power. Avoid feeling you need someone to validate you and become your own source of love, security and approval. You may go through difficult times, lose a job, house, wealth, status or loved ones, but despite all this your personal power can remain intact. Once you become aware of self honouring, you realise that for your own happiness and for you to be truly in a position to help others, you may have to start by reviewing your own needs.

A good place to begin is to start saying no. You will be preserving your energy but in doing so you will have to evaluate your personal boundaries and recognise your own worth.

Have confidence in your body and you will no longer need to seek emotional approval from anyone else. Give yourself positive feedback every day by reflecting on what went well for you and if something went awry, imagine how you could change things. Accept yourself even with your flaws. Aim to do something every day for yourself as this helps to avoid feelings of resentment about responsibilities. Avoid physical clutter and minimise the effects of sensory overload by limiting screen time. Be honest with yourself about your energy levels, take a break and respect your body.

Role Model

Self honouring is not about making a statement that you don't care anymore; it means you will take care of your needs first, which will then enable you to care for others. If others experience rejection, disappointment or simply feel unloved it is a sign that their own inner rules and expectations have been compromised. They may also be afraid or feel scared that perhaps they should start self honouring but aren't ready to take the leap. Just accept and forgive them. Become a role model for others, particularly young children.

Self Honouring Checklist:

- Identify your needs, boundaries and energy levels
- Avoid spreading yourself too thinly
- Be comfortable saying no
- Give yourself permission to take time out and rest
- Become your own source of love and respect
- Set yourself short term self honouring goals and review them regularly

"Fear seems to have many causes.

Fear of loss, fear of failure, fear of being hurt, and so on, but ultimately all fear is the ego's fear of death, of annihilation.

To the ego, death is always just around the corner.

In this mind-identified state, fear of death affects every aspect of your life"

Eckhart Tolle

Chapter 11
Energy Medicine

Recognising that energy is a vital, living, moving force that stimulates the body's own ability to heal itself, energy medicine promotes health, balance and relaxation.

The Japanese developed a system of healing called reiki, Hindu texts described yoga and the chakra systems and traditional Chinese medicine has identified energy channels they call meridians.

Using time-honoured techniques from various ancient cultures, energy practitioners help us to tap into the natural frequencies within our bodies. Working through these super highways of the body, all these healing systems are designed to restore and maintain energy flow, creating balance and harmony. Energy medicine complements other traditional and alternative approaches to medical care and can be used as a system for self-care.

Harmonising Energy

Energy medicine is a very subtle holistic practice that activates the body's own energy systems in order to remove any blockages that may be getting in the way of the body healing itself.

In 1992 Bruce Tainio of Tainio Technology discovered that the average frequency of the human body resonates frequency between 62-72 MHz when healthy. As the frequency drops our immune system is compromised and illness and disease are more likely to develop. The frequency of the human body can be measured by a specialised tool called a biofeedback machine which usually operates by detecting skin temperature, muscle tension and brain wave activity. At the end of this chapter there are some ideas how to raise your vibration.

The Chinese view is that energy, known as chi or qi, not only flows through your body but also surrounds and engulfs you. Therefore, if you can harmonise your energy system you can put your body into the best possible position to heal itself on a physical, mental, emotional and spiritual level.

As a holistic practitioner I have embraced Japanese Reiki, Chinese Qi gong and the ayurvedic healing system from India. Because energy work is not tangible I am often met with curiosity and a certain amount of scepticism. There is little to see during the treatments, although the energy changes are often felt immediately and in the following days.

The Aura

The aura is an electromagnetic energy field that extends and surrounds the human body and other living things for up to a metre. It is believed that the aura is influenced by what we do, our thoughts, places we go and the people we meet as well as reflecting our physical, emotional, mental and spiritual states.

The aura is directly connected to the health of a person and is believed to consist of the following seven layers:

- Physical - this is what you see in the mirror, the physical matter that makes us up. You can touch it and this is where we encounter sickness, ageing and eventually death
- Etheric - this invisible layer is reflected through our meridians and chakras and acts as a double of our physical body as our energy flows through it

- Emotional - reflecting our feelings and emotions, this layer connects us to the past and gives us the opportunity to have emotions, desire and imagination. The keeper of our feelings, this layer can easily become unbalanced, causing blockages and disturbance
- Mental - here we store our belief system and assimilate our thoughts and personal truths. Our conscious mind, intellect and learning belongs here and if unbalanced can reflect mental health issues
- Astral - connected to love and compassion this is said to be the bridge between our physical world and the spiritual realm. All our memories are mirrored here and it is believed that our present and possible futures are also stored in this layer
- Celestial - our intuition and universal love for all resides here, mirroring our subconscious mind
- Causal - this high frequency energy layer is where our soul communicates with our conscious mind through our subconscious mind in our mental layer

Viewing the Aura

Looking too hard defeats the object, gaze rather than stare.

- Sit with your back to a window in a room with natural sunlight
- Sit facing a white wall with little clutter or distractions
- For practise purposes you can use a plant or your own hand
- Close your eyes and relax
- Open your eyes and softly focus on the chosen object
- As you feel your eyes tire, soften your gaze and look past the object
- Any colours you see will be the energetic field of the aura
- Keep practising as it takes time, once you can tune into the energy you will start to see colours
- The more you practise the less you will need a white background

The Chakras

The chakra system was featured in the oldest Sanskrit texts called the Vedas, which originated between 1500 and 500BC and was passed down through oral tradition. Chakras are spinning wheels of energy and it is believed that there are just over a hundred chakras in the human body and that the seven main ones start at the base of the spine running up to the crown at the top of the head. The health of our chakras and the free movement of energy through them is directly connected to the physical body, mind and emotions. You can find more information on the chakras in the aromatherapy chapter.

Explore your chakras with the Chakra Meditation at
www.gaildonnan.com/meditations

Chakra Chart

Name	Location	Mantra	Gland	Issue	Colour
Sahasrara	Crown	OM	Pineal	Understanding, connection to the divine & enlightenment	Violet
Ajna	Third Eye	SHAM	Pineal & Pituitary	Intuition, sense of purpose & psychic senses	Purple
Vishuddha	Throat	HAM	Thyroid	Communication, self expression & healing	Blue
Anahata	Heart	YAM	Heart & Thymus	Love, hope, self acceptance & compassion	Green
Manipura	Solar Plexus	RAM	Pancreas	Energy, vitality and personal power	Yellow
Svadhisthana	Sacral	LAM	Sex Organs & Adrenals	Emotions & sexual intimacy	Orange
Muladhara	Root/Base	VAM	Adrenals	Survival instinct, grounding, sense of belonging & security	Red

Reiki

Reiki, universal life force energy, is about change for the better and finding out what is right for you. Reiki treatments are usually performed with the client laying down, fully clothed on a treatment couch, covered by a blanket. It can also be performed seated or via distance healing. The qualified practitioner may work with a hand placement system sometimes with the addition of a crystal pendulum and a crystal grid.

Reiki addresses the person as a whole, rather than targeting individual symptoms. It can create subtle but meaningful shifts from deep within your own being. On the outside looking in, a Reiki treatment might appear to be merely a sequence of hand placements but it works to restore balance on the deepest possible levels, which may result in the resolution of some health problems, a change in beliefs and attitudes, the ability to make decisions that have been put off or ignored and the realisation of one's true values and priorities in life.

Origins

Reiki was developed by Mikao Usui in the early 20th century and is rooted in Tendai Buddhism and Shinto. The Usui system has been passed through the West through a lineage of teachers and is still used today as a complementary healing system.

Restoring Balance

Reiki works with ki, energy, and encourages its flow through a series of energy channels within the body. Restoring harmony and balance using the body's innate capacity to heal, whilst energising and promoting an overall feeling of wellness, Reiki takes into consideration our mental, physical, spiritual and emotional levels.

Aimed at restoring balance on all levels, Reiki addresses the problem and condition rather than simply masking or relieving symptoms. It creates a deep relaxation that helps the body release stress and tension bringing a sense of peace and calm whilst allowing you to connect to your body as a whole and access your inner wisdom. Reiki dissolves energy blocks and encourages a natural balance between mind, body and spirit. Regular treatments help build up resilience to stress. It can also be used to heal mental or emotional wounds, alleviate panic, fear, frustration, anger, guilt or trauma. Because we spend a lot of time in fight/flight mode, Reiki reminds our physical body how to engage with our parasympathetic nervous system in order to create a calm, self-healing mode which helps the body cleanse itself from toxins while aiding the immune system.

Reiki also has its roots in mindfulness, so it teaches us to live more in the present rather than living in the past or worrying about the future. It can change the way you react to others and improve your self-care techniques.

After experiencing a deep relaxation during the Reiki session, clients often report enjoying a better night's sleep. This return to a more natural state gets the body moving in the right direction to heal itself.

Known to relieve pain, Reiki supports healing by encouraging your system to improve your body's vital functions of breathing, digesting and sleeping, so your physical system is able to function at optimal levels. Reiki helps to relieve pain from migraine and rheumatoid arthritis and can help with symptoms of asthma, chronic fatigue, stress, PMS and insomnia.

Feeling Energy Exercise:

Energy surrounds us. Change your focus on life by spending five minutes a day experiencing and playing with your energy.

- Place your arms in front of you with palms facing each other as if you were holding a beach ball

- Start to bring your palms closer together
- At some point you will start to feel a resistance - this is your own energy field
- Your hands may feel warm, fizz, buzz, pulse or sense a chill

Qi Gong

Originating from traditional Chinese medicine Qi gong is a holistic system of co-ordinated body posture and movement together with breathing exercises and meditation, often used for health, spirituality and martial arts training. Qi signifies life-force energy and gong means skill so Qi gong is the skilful practice of gathering, circulating and applying life-force energy. The human body consists of layers of energy that once understood can be balanced, harmonised and strengthened.

Traditional Chinese medicine believes that our energy body is a template for the physical body and that our emotional energy resonates with our life experiences and personal and professional relationships so that our belief systems become encoded in our cell tissue. All our activity whether it is physical, mental, emotional or spiritual depends on the quality and abundance and free flow of our energy.

Qi gong combines fluid, precise dance like movements, controlled breath and meditation into one routine that encourage the use of your mind's eye to visualise your life energy flowing as you move through space breathing in and out.

Established over 7,000 years ago, according to archaeological evidence, and adopting ancient Chinese philosophies concerning the concepts of energy centres called dantians and meridians, varying Qi gong forms have developed over the years. Traditionally Qi gong training like Reiki was esoteric and secretive with knowledge passed down from master to learner through lineages that kept their own unique methods and interpretations but today this is no longer the case. The growth of Qi gong has grown over centuries and generations but the name wasn't in widespread use until the 20th century.

Dantians

Dantians are a Taoist concept that refer to the three special energy centres in the body where chi is stored.

The lower dantian is the major power house or battery for storing chi and is found two finger widths behind and three fingers below the navel. It is the prime focal point for Qi gong exercises and meditation, and it is our seat of power, vital essence and sexual power.

The middle dantian is located behind the breast bone, level with our hearts. It is the focal point of love, kindness, compassion and the health of our internal organs, especially the heart, lungs and thymus.

The upper dantian is found between our eyebrows, and connects to our intuition, our higher consciousness, and the spiritual aspect of Qi gong.

Meridians

In Chinese philosophy there is no separation from body, mind and spirit, and life is the organisation of the vital life force chi, manifesting in the body, mind and spirit. Meridians work as an energy channel system that carry and distribute chi, they are not blood vessels and have no anatomical channel structure so you cannot see them.

There are twelve main meridians in the body, each associated with five elements and Chinese medicine organ systems which are listed in yin and yang pairs. Yin and yang is a Chinese philosophy which describes how opposite forces may actually be complementary, interconnected, and interdependent in the natural world, and how they may give rise to each other as they interrelate to one another. Chi should flow continuously from one meridian to another and any break in the flow is an indication of imbalance. In Qi gong, restoring the chi to its natural flow is the goal to restoring health and wellbeing.

Chi energy points cannot be felt until enough energy is built up in the lower dantian. Energy then travels through the meridians to the other dantian points and lends them their sensation. In martial arts terms this is known as the centre of power. Going to a regular class or performing the exercises daily will increase the energy through posture, breathing, co-ordinating movements with the breath and moving the energy internally with intent.

Maintaining Health

Qi gong is great for any age or fitness level but especially suited to our older generation as the exercises can be adapted and is more commonly forming part of the care plan for the elderly worldwide. Offering an efficient and powerful way to maintain health with gentle minimum impact, it's easy on the joints and can be done by people who cannot access other forms of aerobic exercise or yoga.

By increasing the supply and flow of energy throughout the body, it harmonises, strengthens and heals internal organs. Qi gong claims to have rejuvenating effects on the body and is believed to increase longevity of life as well as inducing calm emotional states. The movements focus on gently opening and stretching the joints and muscles of the body therefore releasing tension while increasing the flow of blood and energy and nourishing all parts of the body.

Energy Exercise to try on your own:

- Rub your hands together to cause friction
- Slowly move your hands apart to feel the energy you have created

Energy Exercise to try with a partner:

- Sit or stand two arms-length away facing each other
- Ask your partner to close their eyes and take a deep breath
- Relax your shoulders and back muscles
- Imagine chi rising from the earth into your body
- When you sense this energy, ask your partner to extend an arm towards you with the palm facing downward
- Slowly raise your own arm until your palm is within a few inches of their palm
- Using your mind, direct the chi through your body until it passes along your arms and out of your fingertips to theirs
- You should both have a sense of the energy passing through, it may feel tingly

Chi Prayer Hands:

- Extend your hands in line with your solar plexus, place hands together in a prayer position, close your eyes and begin deep breathing
- As you exhale slowly move your palms slightly apart, continue inhaling and exhaling
- When you are ready, turn one palm slightly downward and one slightly upward, continue inhaling and exhaling slowly
- Feel the chi/energy building
- Play with your hand movements by moving them further apart in all directions
- Squeeze and release as you feel the energy force between your hands
- Return to starting position
- Move your palms upwards as you inhale and downwards as you exhale, this bow action connects you to earth chi

If you are stressed, anxious, or physically drained, a Reiki energy healing session or practising Qi gong can help you relax and feel more balanced. It's important to note that energy healing is a complementary therapy that shouldn't exclude any Western medicine you may be taking and Reiki is best carried out in a course of three treatments.

Increase your energy level with the Energy Meditation at www.gaildonnan.com/meditations

Tips for raising your vibration:

- Light a candle
- Diffuse aromatherapy oils such as Rose (320MHz), Helichrysum (180MHz), Frankincense (147MHz), Lavender (118MHz), Chamomile (105MHz), Juniper (98MHz), Sandalwood (98MHz), Peppermint (78MHz)
- Practise gratitude and kindness
- Eat more raw, organic unprocessed food
- Eat fresh and dried herbs
- Take an Epsom salt bath
- Enjoy a Yoga class
- Infuse your drinking water with citrus fruits and herbs
- Practise positive thought
- Meditate
- Begin a Qigong discipline
- Spend time in nature
- Enjoy a reiki session
- Practise present moment awareness
- Have digital detox time

Tracy's Story

Lost - adrift on a turbulent sea of self-doubt and without any idea of what I was going to do now...

That is the best way to describe the mess that was me on the day I first met Gail. It was quite by chance, a quirk of fate - although I now know there is no such thing. As the quote says "When the student is ready, the teacher will appear" Buddha Siddartha Guatama.

I had taught in primary and out of school education since leaving university, other than a break while my children were babies, in one form or another. It was what I did, teach.

But over the course of the previous year I had become increasingly at odds with the system that was putting children, the individuals with all the promise, energy and imagination of youth, into tidy little boxes that squashed their individual gifts and true natures. It was killing me. Literally. As was the fact that not just myself and my health, but ultimately my family, and my marriage were suffering. I never saw them, I was either at school, often putting in long, long days or squirrelled away in my ever-expanding home office space trying to fill in exhaustive paperwork which in the long run did not benefit the children in my care. I threw microwave food at my own children, missed their plays and sporting achievements. It was not living - I was hollow from the giving of myself, relied heavily on grandparents who were mercifully close and began to resent the fact that family life was stopping me getting my work done - If I could just make it to the weekend, the half term holiday and summer all would be ok. It wasn't, and inevitably when these much-awaited times came, I was ill, really ill, and so still not able to share the family time as I had promised.

The straw that broke the camel's back was my daughter who was six at the time, knocking with some trepidation on my office door. I sighed - "what now?" I thought. I recall I didn't even look up from my screen where I had retreated, meal on a plate, having served up yet more microwave food, some hours before. I resisted the urge to say what I was thinking and instead - "Mummy's just busy darling, I won't be long" (yeah right!).

"Mummy, I know you are busy, you don't have to read to me tonight, night-night" she turned to leave as my heart tore in two - I'm crying now at the memory. Her little head was low as she clutched her Eeyore and toddled off to bed. She was just six. What on earth was I doing?

Within a week I'd handed my notice in, supported to some degree by my husband, but what now? I only knew the path I had walked for so many years. I was scared for the future. What would I do? Would we have enough money? What would people think? Would I ever work again? - I only knew teaching. It had consumed my life - no time for hobbies and interests, family or friends. Some months later, scrolling through Facebook I chanced upon a post from a friend who was attending one of Gail's Vision Boarding workshops. There was a place left, so I went with her, more to have a catch up than anything. I had absolutely no expectations and no idea the significance of this sunny spring day in Ripon. Nervously I listened as the others attending introduced themselves, say what they did and what they were hoping to get from the day. My heart was racing and my palms sweaty - what was I going to say? What would they think? These ladies all seemed so "together". They had purpose - I was floating helplessly from one day to the next - and planning on making an excuse and running for the door. I felt sick. My turn - I can't even remember what garbage I came out with, I just know that when I did finally make eye contact with Gail, she smiled. A non-judgemental smile of encouragement. From that moment on, I knew I was in an environment that would support me, and that I was ready to find my path, find myself. But how?

That was some time ago now. Looking back, it feels like a lifetime ago and a world away. "Wow, look at you; you look so well", old friends say when I see them. And it's true, I feel it, I am so truly grateful to have been in that bleak place, and to have found Gail, and returned to myself.

My life is so different now. I am my own boss, having opened Breathing Space in February this year. I work from home so work fits around family life rather than the other way around and I have been to all my daughters' school plays, recitals and sports days. I love the fact that I can use my skill set to help people that are in need, and really make a difference without compromising my integrity as I had done for so many years. I am at last present in my own existence – and that is huge!

I have attended many workshops at the Mindfulspace Wellbeing Studios and never fail to grow from the experiences offered there, shared with like-minded people, in a fantastically encouraging environment. I have studied my Reiki 1st and 2nd Degrees with Gail, a truly incredible and life changing experience which has helped rebuild my health, and well-being, but also my business. I studied my Reiki and Indian head massage with Gail. I am looking to add a holistic facial certificate to my collection and am currently studying for my mindfulness diploma which has been a journey in self-discovery as well as, a re-affirmation of my values and hopes for our shared futures. I just love being at the Mindfulspace Wellbeing Studios and cannot wait to discover and learn more. I swear that you do not have to say or do anything whilst there - just an hour or so of being immersed in Gail's presence and a deep feeling of peace, understanding and knowledge just soaks into your entire being - like some sort of osmosis.

I am very much a work in progress, but now I am my life's work. Life is now so fulfilling and rewarding, and every day teaches me something new. Gail has a way of teaching which speaks to people on all levels and makes the entire experience inspiring and uplifting. I cannot recommend both Gail, and the studios highly enough, nor express the gratitude I feel to her and the wonderful people that I have been fortunate to meet thanks to my "chance" encounter whilst lost at sea.

Thank you Gail - with all my heart xx
Breathing Space, Thirsk, North Yorkshire

"Reiki is love, love is
wholeness, wholeness is
balance, balance is wellbeing,
wellbeing is freedom from
disease"

Mikau Usui

Chapter 12
Mindfulness

Mindfulness is the mental state achieved by focussing our awareness on the present moment, while acknowledging and accepting our feelings, thoughts and physical sensations without judgement.

Mindfulness has existed for centuries, at least since 500BC with its roots deeply planted in Eastern philosophies from India, Ancient Nepal, Tibet, China and Japan. Mindfulness and meditation are principle teachings in Buddhism and form part of the Four Noble Truths and the Eightfold Path to enlightenment. Affecting what we say, do and think, mindfulness focuses our attention on being fully aware of our thoughts and actions, whilst developing wisdom through the encouragement of compassion and non-judgement. In the East, where goals and lifestyles are very different to those in the Western world, mindfulness is taught as a way of life.

Pause for Thoughts

You may often hear the phrase "being in the moment" associated with mindfulness. This is the ability to be aware of your thoughts, physical sensations, emotions and behaviours. Mindfulness gives us time to come up with a wise response to the difficulties we often face in our lives, because it teaches us to become aware of the urge to instantly react, offering us the chance to make a more considered and creative decision about the way we want to behave.

A major mindfulness technique encourages us to sit with our uncomfortable thoughts and feelings just a little longer than usual, to give a space between our automatic impulses, our jumps to conclusions or auto-pilot reactions. As humans we tend to employ our same learnt emotional response when faced with situations. Mindfulness offers us the opportunity to pause and consider our actions. Constant repetition of regular mindfulness and meditation practices can help to re-program our brains, increasing our resilience and promoting feelings of happiness and purpose.

Increased Awareness

Most of our anxieties are rooted in the past. Living mindfully can change our relationship with previous experiences and remove habits and reactions that have been laid down in the neural pathways of our brain. Teaching us to observe our thoughts, including those unhelpful re-occurring ones, and allowing them to pass without reaction can bring added peace and calm to our busy lives.

Many of us have become addicted to being busy, perhaps because it gives us an excuse to bury difficult emotions. Don't be fooled into thinking mindfulness eliminates stress, it simply makes us more aware. Mindfulness teaches that the solution is not to detach from our challenging emotions; it encourages us to engage gently with them in order to better manage the feelings and behaviours that they arouse.

Connect with the Physical

One of the main concepts of mindfulness is to remain in the present moment and be able to identify how you are feeling from moment to moment, whether it be happy, sad, fearful, angry, or some other emotion. It's a heightened awareness of what's going on both inside and out of ourselves. Using our ability to connect with the physical – the feel of the pavement, the smell of the flowers or simply the touch of another's hand moves ourselves out of our heads and into our bodies where we stop reacting from a fear perspective and learn not to take our thoughts so seriously.

Empowerment

Mindfulness adapts and changes our mind-set, re-writing how we interpret and process our life events, both good and bad, and it reminds us that we are more than the sum of our current circumstances.

At a low point in my life mindfulness helped me move to a more empowered, happier way of life. Giving me permission to examine my emotions, including the difficult ones, in order to process them rather than continue hoarding them. Instructing me to stop judging myself and others, and guiding me towards compassion and gratitude.

Mindfulness Exercise - Head to Heart

The mindfulness head to heart exercise is a great way to identify any pathways that may be creating emotional pain for us.

- Sit quietly and comfortably
- Think of a situation which has caused you emotional pain, anger, sadness or fear
- Sit with the feelings that situation brings for a few minutes
- Try and identify where it is felt in the body and what those feelings are
- Now identify the emotions those feelings bring

I first encountered this exercise during my mindfulness studies, I identified that I felt a huge tightness and sadness in my chest when thinking about the sad and untimely death of a dear friend. Giving myself permission to identify what emotion was sitting there, I felt a lot of anger. Anger is frequently the first emotional reaction we all have. I was angry that as a fixer in life, I didn't fix her. She was taken from us by cancer and there was nothing I could do. I felt totally powerless.

The minute I identified the emotion living inside me, the tears came thick and fast, pouring down my cheeks and I had never felt so alive with raw emotion. After ten minutes, I began to feel so much better, almost lighter and was then asked to identify other deeper emotions that were buried under the anger. I then recognised the loneliness, guilt, frustration, heartbreak and denial.

Our thoughts generate emotions that should generally last around ninety seconds but because we fight, resist, block or even build on them they hang around much longer. In my case I had been carrying all those emotions around for over three years. This head to heart exercise gave me freedom and I was able to begin to accept my friend's untimely death.

Ego and Mindfulness

The word ego comes from the Latin for I, and reflects our self-esteem and self-image. In psychoanalysis it is defined as part of the mind that mediates between the conscious and unconscious and is responsible for reality testing and our sense of personal identity. Ego impacts on impulse control, character development, interpersonal relationships and cognitive processing and disconnects us from our intuition, authentic self and spiritual side.

Our ego not only helps us see and react to the world we live in, but also determines how we think the world should see us. Most of us raised in a western culture already have some expectation of becoming a shining example of how we are supposed to be. Ego is the who and what of your thoughts about yourself and on this level, it is benign.

Unfortunately, ego often has a companion – the inner critic, that little self-sabotaging voice constantly chattering inside you offering criticism and commentary on your thoughts and actions. This pair form part of the conscious thinking mind and are responsible for many of the knee jerk reactions and crazy decisions that cause us much unhappiness.

Together they are responsible for resistance to the situations we find ourselves in versus where we think we should be – creating an imagined and impassable gulf. These incongruities lead to self-doubt and anxiety. Mindfulness teaches us to remove or pay little attention to our ego and its companion the inner critic.

Awareness

Mindfulness works by encouraging us to relinquish the ego, the inner critic and the conscious thinking mind and neutralise the impact of the contents of our own minds, and not to take our thoughts too seriously. Removing the need to live in our heads, mindfulness teaches us how to work with feelings and emotions as they arise, exploring how they feel in our body rather than in our mind. This is why the head to heart exercise is so beneficial because once you can identify these feelings and emotions without adding drama you will be able to process them effectively. This state is a cornerstone of mindfulness referred to as "awareness".

If you regularly complete the head to heart exercises you may start to see a pattern emerging of similar words or emotions which suggests that your sense of self is obscuring the way you look out onto the world and perhaps how you think the world sees you. Regular practice of this exercise replaces unhelpful reactions with 'awareness'.

Make Friends with your Ego and Inner Critic

- Notice when you are reacting to situations in an emotional way
- Think about how it feels in your body
- Notice when you are being self-critical
- Record the words and tone of voice used when you are self-critical
- Do they remind you of someone in your past that was critical of you?

- Interact and make friends with your inner critic - "I know you are worried about me and feel unsafe, however you are causing me unnecessary pain." Talk to your inner critic and ego with kindness and compassion as you would to a friend
- Find something your inner critic, ego and your compassionate self can agree on. "I know it would be good to have cooked an evening meal, however that is not the way it is now, let's make do with what's in the cupboard"
- Start keeping a journal to record your progress

Non Judgement

Mindfulness is also about non judgment and compassion for ourselves and others. Judging is a natural component of human nature and the need to judge usually stems from fear. These fears could perhaps arise because we feel inadequate or inferior, so we criticise and judge in order to help ourselves feel better. Judgement is a big energy drainer, so the less judgmental we are the more open and loving we become.

If I notice myself judging someone, I congratulate myself on my awareness, I then create a loving stance by smiling at the person. This immediately inserts a pause in my judgemental thoughts and gives me the ability for compassion.

Compassion

Compassion is being kind, having empathy, tolerance, understanding of yourself and others. Self-compassion gives us a better emotional balance when we are stressed. Your attitude to yourself often impacts on your attitude towards others; compassion sees behind the human being and its flaws. Remind yourself that you are important and constantly tell yourself that you do not have to be perfect but you are simply a work in progress, and that is good enough.

Treat yourself to the Loving Kindness Meditation at www.gaildonnan.com/meditations

Gratitude

Gratitude is a simple way of bringing the focus of your life back to what is really important. When I venture too far off this track, something generally happens to steer me back to gratitude. If we experience the death of someone close to or undertake the care of a loved one with a long-term illness, it makes us realise that not much else matters apart from our health and we can express gratitude for this.

Gratitude teaches awareness and grounding, it celebrates all that we appreciate and brings us back to a much simpler existence where the minutiae of life is really not worth getting upset about. At night, just as I am going off to sleep I remind myself what has gone well for me that day and all the things I am grateful for.

For the last few years I have kept a gratitude jar and when I feel really grateful for something I write it down and put it in my jar, my daughter also has one in her bedroom and every New Year we empty the jars and enjoy reading the contents together.

Living Mindfully

Living mindfully is the best way to really change your life in positive ways.

- Performing random acts of kindness is a great thing to do, if you have children ask them for their ideas as they can be really inventive
- Try to give up the need to always be right and go a day without complaining or criticising
- Be confident in who you are, you don't have to impress others
- Lessen your time on social media

- Go outdoors and spend time exercising in nature
- Take a break from the need to control or blame others and avoid taking ownership of other people's dramas
- Give up your limiting beliefs and self-defeating talk
- Embrace change rather than resist it, you never know where it will take you
- Give up living your life to other peoples' expectations
- Do something creative
- Have a rest for ten minutes without feeling guilty
- Listen to people without planning your reply or trying to solve their problems
- Keep a gratitude journal by your bed and fill it in every night before you go to sleep
- Accept happiness is not meant to be a constant state
- Avoid resisting against any problems that arise in your life
- Give up feeling entitled to a life free of suffering

Mindful Eating Exercise

This exercise is great for children and can spark some interesting discussion and learning.

- Eat your food at a table without distractions such as the television, phone or tablet
- Take one mouthful of the food
- Put your cutlery down
- Eat slowly paying attention to the colour, smell, sound, temperature, flavour, texture and taste, while thinking about the origin of the food

Mindful Listening Exercise

Without realising, most of us listen to others waiting for a space in the conversation in which to contribute with either our own agenda or to offer a fix for the problem. Mindful or active listening is a communication technique which involves giving the other person 100% of our attention, constantly noticing ourselves waiting for our turn to speak and returning our attention to the speaker in order to truly listen to what they have to say.

- Sit facing your partner, look into their eyes and decide who will be the speaker and who the listener
- Listen attentively to what they are saying
- Notice when you want to interject
- Bring your attention back to listening
- If you really want to say something, reflect back what you have heard or ask neutral questions, "I heard you say… is that right?" or "Is there more?"
- Now swap roles with the listener becoming the speaker

Kim's Story

It was March 2017 when I finally plucked up the courage to send a Facebook message to Gail asking for the help I had needed for a long time. Since starting University in 2002 I had been trying to manage anxiety, low self-esteem and a dysfunctional relationship with food by myself with only a brief dalliance with CBT (Cognitive Behavioural Therapy). It was time to get brave, and after starting yoga at the Mindfulspace Wellbeing Studios I knew I would be comfortable there, in their calm surroundings, and hopefully start a new journey. Little did I know that this meeting would change my life. The program introduced me to meditation and mindfulness and from then on it has been a daily part of my life. At the end of one specific meditation I remember laying there almost crying with relief that I had finally found a way to help, and I knew I wanted to learn more. Mindfulness and meditation had started to make a difference to me and I wanted to spread this magic elsewhere, and so embarked upon the meditation teacher training. Starting this course just shows how far I had already come as previously I would never do anything by myself and now here I was reading a meditation in front of three other people! This course discussed the different parts and the effects of meditation on the brain. This ignited a spark and I then completed the mindfulness diploma. These courses are interesting and taught in such a way they are easy to understand but also with an element of self-exploration. Completing these courses taught me about myself as well as mindfulness. I can't rate the program or the courses highly enough. With the help of Gail and these courses I started Zen Warriors and now teach mindfulness and meditation to children. Helping the younger generation to learn the tools that will help them as they navigate through life's ups and downs… just like Gail helped me.

"Be happy for no reason like a child. If you are happy for a reason, you're in trouble, because that reason can be taken from you"

Deepak Chopra

Chapter 13
Meditation

Meditation is a technique for resting the mind and finding the silence and peace that resides within ourselves. There is no right or wrong way to meditate; each experience will be different on different days. If you worry about doing it right, then it becomes counterproductive. There are many different types of meditation and it is an extremely personal journey which will lead you to what feels right for you. I was drawn to guided and moving meditation and so I trained in both those techniques and now teach meditation, taking regular groups and circles and running accredited courses supporting others to become meditation teachers.

The Silence Inside

If I was to sum up what meditation means to me personally, it is purely about creating an awareness of me in that moment by finding the silence that exists inside. Meditation can be anything that frees up my mind from other distractions, such as unwanted thoughts. By listening to sounds or focusing on my breathing, I go into 'the gap', which is a state of consciousness deep inside and into a place between thought and sleep. I like to think of it as myself in 'neutral'.

Once in this place, you are able to notice your thoughts without identifying or building on them and can begin to understand that these are just sensory movements that you can let come and go without attaching any drama to them. Meditation is not about trying to block or reject thought, it is about being aware of thoughts as they arise, examining them and then letting go.

Although meditation is not religious, a large number of religions do practise it, including Buddhism from 500BC, Sufi/Islam, Hinduism, Christianity, Pagan, Judaism and Taoism.

Advantages

Meditation develops concentration, focus, positivity, clarity, a sense of calm and the ability to see the true nature of things. During meditation our bodies produce the feel-good chemicals, endorphins and serotonin, which are essential to our well-being. Endorphins are our natural pain killers and also boost our immune system.

Meditation can reduce levels of stress and anxiety by triggering the parasympathetic nervous system inducing relaxation, it lowers blood pressure while increasing blood flow to the brain and can promote deep sleep.

Creativity is often increased as you tap into your higher self and tune into your intuition, purpose and spiritual direction while opening your mind to new ideas. Meditation helps me find the calmness within, regardless of what is going on around me and a ten-minute meditation will re-charge my energy.

Practice

Meditation improves with practise. Start with a couple of minutes and build up gradually. Set a timer for one minute and look at the leaf on the opposite page until the timer goes off. If you have any thoughts unrelated to the picture, simply notice them and return your focus to the picture. Gradually increase the time as it feels right. Begin a meditation journal to support your meditative practices; a place where you can capture your thoughts, record your efforts and track your progress.

Start with the Five Minute Meditation at www.gaildonnan.com/meditations

Once you have worked through all the meditations there are plenty of free apps and podcasts available for download - see the further listening section.

Types of Meditation

Finding the right technique is very personal; try and explore as many methods as you can.

Guided Meditation

A good place to start, especially if you are new to meditation. Simply follow the oral instructions and you will be guided from start to finish. If a visualisation is included then it allows you to create an uplifting mental picture and then concentrate on it for a period of time.

When focusing on positive experiences, your body relaxes allowing a sense of joy and balance by harnessing and stimulating those feelings. With all meditation, the more you practice the stronger the pathways in the brain become. Generating strong, positive feelings on a regular basis allows changes to occur naturally.

Walking Meditation

Mindful walking is a Taoist moving meditation which stills your inner compass and lowers brain waves so you feel more relaxed and clear headed. When we are in a highly emotional state we become less able to think clearly as we are functioning from the ancient reptilian part of our brains, our nerve cells are inflamed and walking helps to distract us and activate other areas of our brain. Walking meditations are a real favourite of mine because they are done on the move.

Mantra Meditations

Mantra comes from the Sanskrit meaning sacred message or charm. It is a word, sound or calming phrase that is repeated in order to aid concentration during meditation. Some popular Buddhist mantras are;

- Om - according to Hindu belief is the sound that created the world
- Om shanti - Peace - this is a favourite of mine
- Sita ram - opening your heart to celebrate love

Transcendental Meditation

This derives from simple natural Hindu traditions; where the meditator silently repeats a personally assigned mantra, which can be a word, sound or phrase, typically devoid of meaning. Your mantra is usually given to you from a teacher or guide and is designed to allow your body to settle in a state of peace without using concentration or effort.

Mindful Walking Mediation Exercise (15 minutes):

- As you are walking, pay attention to things with a childlike curiosity as if you were noticing them for the first time
- When ready, move onto observing your thoughts - don't block or reject them
- Now, spend some time rhythmically breathing and stepping
- Breathe in for three steps and out for four steps (adjust as needed)
- When ready, listen to the sounds around you for a few minutes
- Continue walking noticing the things you are drawn to
- Zoom your vision in and out of objects that are near or in the distance
- Finally stop and take a break
- Stand still for three minutes and notice how you feel

Breathing Meditation Exercise (3 minutes):

- Take three deep breaths in and out
- Repeat in your mind "I am breathing in and I am breathing out and I recognise that worries have no place in meditation"

Short Walking Meditation Exercise:

- Focus your mind on the mechanics of walking
- Take slow steady steps feeling the ground beneath you
- Be aware of the sounds you make as your foot meets the ground
- Look at everything with a childlike curiosity

Breathing Meditation:

- Find a quiet place where you will be undisturbed
- Switch off your phone
- Sit or lie comfortably
- Close your eyes slowly or have a fixed gaze
- Take three deep breaths in
- Purposely tense parts of the body and then let them go starting at the feet
- Notice the rhythm of the breath without trying to change it
- Mentally trace the outline of your body starting at the feet
- Keep noticing the rhythm of the breath without trying to change it
- Scan the body and mentally note any tense or aching areas of the body
- Breathe into the tensions and relax
- Breathe into the aches and relax
- If any thoughts come to mind, don't hold onto them, don't build on them just let them pass
- If your mind wanders, because it will, that's what minds do, just keep bringing your attention back to your breathing

- Notice the in and out journey of the breath and the second where the in breath meets the out breath. In that second there is a gap, a peaceful moment where nothing happens
- That is you without thought
- Let that quieten you and centre you, perhaps allow that gap to travel through the in breath and back out through the out breath
- When it feels right for you, bring your attention back to your body where it rests
- Spend a while reflecting on what you appreciate and are grateful for
- As the meditation draws to a close, begin to move through the senses. First go to hearing, what can you hear, smell, what can you smell, taste, swallow or move your tongue around the mouth, movement, make small movements with your hands and your feet, perhaps stretch and finally on an in breath open your eyes

This Breathing Meditation can be found at www.gaildonnan.com/meditations

Linda's Story

I'm a firm believer that the universe sends you what you need, and this is how meditation came into my life in a big way. Until that point I knew about meditation and enjoyed group meditations when I encountered them as part of self-development courses. But to be honest it wasn't something I practiced on a regular basis. Certainly, whenever I flew I popped myself into a meditative trance to cope with my trauma at take-off and when landing and I tended to zone out during long transatlantic flights to help deal with my nervousness about flying, but that was almost the limit of my use of meditative practices.

In 2007 I was diagnosed with breast cancer, which came as a big shock as until then the big C hadn't touched our family. At one of my early appointments I picked up a CD which was lying amongst the plethora of Macmillan literature and living healthily pamphlets. It was by natural energy healer Ruth Kaye and was a CD designed to help relaxation and encourage healing sleep. Consisting of a series of guided meditations interspersed with relaxing music, this CD became my companion during this time and in the following years as I came to term with my illness, surgery and recovery. My husband thoughtfully copied it onto my phone so that whenever anxieties arose and threatened to overwhelm or sleep eluded me, out would come the earphones and I would plug into Ruth's soothing voice. The universe had indeed sent me what I needed.

A few years later I was diagnosed with a life-threatening blood cancer – leukaemia and I was admitted to St James Hospital in Leeds. This time it was really serious – two years to live kind of serious – and the universe decided I needed something more than a CD to help me through, so it sent me a raft of remarkable doctors and the wonderful Ruth Kaye in person. Cancer not only invades the body it also takes over your mind. Recognising this, the oncology department at St James' takes a more holistic approach and has on offer a range of complementary therapies, including massage, aromatherapy, reflexology and meditation, which go alongside the conventional medical approach. And natural energy healer Ruth, with her healing hands and magic words, was part of this. Her weekly visits to me during the almost three years I eventually spent in hospital certainly aided my recovery and together, through meditation we created a powerful source of energy and healing that worked with the powerful and toxic chemicals that were needed to kill the cancerous cells. During this time with Ruth's guidance, I experienced some of the deepest and most calming meditations. These are places that I still return to now, seven years later when anxiety threatens to overwhelm me, or whenever life gets a little out of kilter.

I would like to think that mediation has now become part of what I do, but I'm human and I forget or allow stuff to get in the way. However, I'm getting much better at recognising when I'm feeling unbalanced and need some restorative meditative time. Attending Gail's regular mediation circle at the Mindfulspace Wellbeing Company studios helps to keep me balanced and on-track.

"Get out of your head and get into your heart.
Think less and feel more"

Osho

Chapter 14
Ayurveda & Yoga

Yoga and ayurveda are two inter-linked branches of an old tradition originating from the Indian subcontinent known today as Vedic knowledge.

Used together, or on their own, they can both offer considerable benefits for our health and well-being.

Ayurveda

Ayurveda (pronounced ay-ur-vay-da) is a holistic science of living well. Developed more than 3,000 years ago in ancient India, its fundamental principle is that health and wellness depend on a delicate balance between the mind, body, and spirit and that we can make use of our intuition and the body's own wisdom to become our own personal healer, staying vibrant and healthy whilst realising our full human potential.

I first came across ayurveda in the late 90s, since then I have trained in two ayurvedic therapies, Indian head massage and hot stone/chakra therapy. For many years I taught both in further education and am still a practising therapist and teacher in both these fields.

Self-Healing

The two main guiding principles of ayurveda are the mind and body being connected, and that nothing has more power to heal and transform the body than the mind.

It is believed that freedom from illness depends upon expanding our own awareness, bringing it into balance, and then extending that balance to the body. In ayurveda, practices such as meditation and yoga help to balance the body, which being thought inseparable from the mind, lead to both mental and physical wellness.

An example of this is that during a meditation or relaxing treatment you would effortlessly enter a state of expanded awareness and inner quiet which refreshes the mind and body, restoring balance to both.

Yoga

The Oxford English Dictionary definition of yoga reads, "a Hindu spiritual and ascetic discipline, a part of which, including breath control, simple meditation, and the adoption of specific bodily postures, is widely practised for health and relaxation."

Today yoga is mostly associated with physical postures (asanas) though this is only one aspect of yogic philosophy and practice.

The Sanskrit word prana refers to energy or life-force and yoga poses, asanas, and associated breath work are designed to move blocked prana through the subtle body. According to yogic and Hindu tradition, the subtle body, also referred to as the energy body, is a part of you that you cannot see or touch - it is where your energy flows. When energy becomes blocked in a chakra, it triggers physical, mental, or emotional imbalances that manifest in symptoms such as anxiety, lethargy, or poor digestion.

Yoga asanas are designed to free up energy and stimulate any imbalanced chakras and this can in turn create internal shifts. A good instructor will show you how you can tune into your chakras to harness your power and then how to shift your energy in a new direction.

Benefits

Yoga is great for reducing stress and allows for greater relaxation. The physical benefits of yoga range from increased flexibility, strength, balance, stamina, body alignment and reduced joint pain. The mental benefits of yoga bring stress reduction, body awareness, better sleep, improved self-confidence and relaxation.

If you use yoga as a workout regime, flexibility and strength can be gained, plus you may even lose weight or tone up. Because yoga also has a spiritual philosophy behind it, it can become both a passion and a spiritual way of life. As there are several methods and types of yoga, it is a case of trying them and deciding what feels right for you. I practice a few yoga asanas every morning along with a short energy moving meditation.

I have a friend who is a yoga instructor so I asked her to put into words what yoga means to her.

"I have been in the fitness industry since the age of seventeen, teaching aerobics, step, circuits etc... I found yoga while living in Dubai at my local large chain gym. My first downward facing dog felt like hell even though I was fairly fit and strong this discipline really pushed me. I chose the power type yoga classes as I was only interested in how much stronger and flexible I would become. This really hurts me to write, but when the Instructor said if you would like to leave before savasana (relaxation part of yoga) I always did, thinking it was not important.

The more I practised the more I began to understand what yoga was about, having moments of clarity, calmness and sometimes emotional breakdowns during my practice. I was struggling with where I was living, with my job and career path plus being a new Mum. Yoga helped me to keep calm in my head, not to overthink and how to deal with surprises that come up in life a lot better than I had been.

We made the decision to bring our family to the UK, once the children were settled I could concentrate on my direction. Very foolishly I thought I was too old to retrain as a yoga Instructor and worried about putting myself out there, but I took the plunge. As for savasana, now I cannot wait for that bit when I practice myself and believe it is the most important part of the practice. Finding peace and giving myself time to totally slow down brings so much to me that I can give others my patience and time. I hope I pass this onto everyone I teach. I still love the anatomical aspect of teaching but teaching yoga and seeing what it brings to the students in so many different ways makes me so happy and fulfilled in my work. I cannot wait to continue to learn the art of yoga for many years to come in continued education and loving the pleasure of passing onto others."

Nicola Lymer
Exhale Fitness

Amy's Story

Following the Manchester Arena terrorist attack in May 2017 I was diagnosed with PTSD (Post Traumatic Stress Disorder). I became extremely anxious, I couldn't sleep without nightmares, I was on high alert at all times suffering panic attacks from loud noises. My life became a living hell. I allowed myself to be consumed with anxiety and rarely went out. The life I had known had been taken over.

I had received counselling and seen many professionals but nothing seemed to really give me just what I was looking for until I discovered yoga. It was from here slowly things began to change. It did not happen over-night, but the yoga studio and the practice began to be my sanctuary and I rebuilt a strength from within using yoga. My body at this stage was very weak and fragile but my mind began to grow in strength, in time so did my body. I began to bring my focus to me and only me and realised how special I was and how my body and me needed looking after. My amazing yoga teacher helped me to gain my strength, physically and mentally. Not by pushing me to do more, but to find my own balance.

Yoga has become a very large part of my life and I have made many new friends and I have found my happy place. I have never considered myself to be the sporty or spiritual type, in fact I've never in all honesty had a type or even really a hobby. For me yoga is the most fun, satisfying, relaxing, self-finding new hobby and I would highly recommend it. Not just to people suffering from trauma but to absolutely anyone; I feel everyone in some way, young or old would benefit from yoga.

"Real peace is unshakable.
Bliss is unchanged by
gain or loss"

Yogi Bhajan

Chapter 15
Aromatherapy

Aromatherapy is the science and art of using aromatic plant extracts for healing and cosmetic purposes. These extracts, known as essential oils, are highly concentrated and are used therapeutically, either singly or blended, to improve our physical, mental and spiritual well-being. Essential oils that calm the mind or lift our mood have been used for thousands of years with holistic therapies, yoga and meditation.

Essential Oils

There are over a hundred essential oils and each one has a unique chemistry, resulting in their anti-inflammatory, pain-relieving, decongesting, antifungal, cleansing, antiseptic, antibacterial and mood lifting properties. The sources of essential oils differ from plant to plant. Extracted in different processes these oils may come from peel or pith, resin, seeds, leaves, roots, bark and flowers.

Mood Enhancing

Aromatherapy works mainly through our sense of smell. These essential oil molecules travel to the top of the nose where they come into contact with olfactory nerve cells which have tiny hairs that can recognise a specific aroma. Scientists think that the activity of the nerve signal passing through this area alters our brain chemistry creating a change in our mood.

Our sense of smell is the oldest of all our senses and it is linked to some of the most ancient and deepest parts of the brain. As we breathe in, the aromas of essential oils trigger our brains to produce both emotional and physical responses.

In addition, as we inhale these essential oils they enter our respiratory system and become absorbed by our bodies. Those oils with antibacterial, antiseptic and antiviral properties, eucalyptus, sage, rosemary and tea-tree for example, help the sinuses, throat and chest and relieve symptoms of infections and allergies.

Medicinal Properties

Most essential oils have medicinal properties, which can alleviate pain, relax muscles, heal wounds, aid digestion and fight colds and flu. Use rosemary in a diffuser to reduce levels of the stress hormone cortisol and inhale calming rose oil to lower adrenaline levels. Clary sage, fennel, basil and geranium have a hormone balancing effect too. Lavender, geranium and citrus oils are especially useful for "women's complaints" as they offer all round benefits, that's not to say that men can't use them too.

Once an essential oil enters the bloodstream it is carried to all areas of the body. The majority of essential oils leave the body within hours, mainly through excretion via the kidneys, although their effects can last much longer within the tissues.

Positive Effects

Dependant on their properties essential oils can either relax or stimulate us. Oils are classified into three categories or notes - top, middle and base, and each category has a different effect on the body and brain. Some notes work on well-being and mood, concentration and focus while others address relaxation, balance and energy.

Top notes are stimulating mood up-lifters, these are usually light and airy and disappear quickly into the air. They don't linger and typically last one to two hours. Top notes include, eucalyptus, citrus and the mint oils.

Middle notes form the majority of all essential oils and have a good balancing effect. They are normally warm fragrances that last anywhere from two to five hours and add body to a blend of oils. Black pepper, geranium, palmarosa, lavender, pine and rosemary are all middle note essential oils.

Base note oils are heavy and often more expensive than other oils. They are inclined to remain around for a longer time, lasting from one to five days or more. Base note oils are found in cedarwood, frankincense, patchouli, rose, sandalwood, vetiver and ylang ylang.

Using Essential Oils

As essential oils are highly concentrated and volatile they need to be diluted before use. Dilution prolongs the beneficial effects of the oil as it prevents it from evaporating too fast allowing it more time to be absorbed. It is recommended that undiluted essential oils are not used directly on the skin to prevent irritation and toxicity. Some of the best ways of enjoying essential oils include:

Diffusers

These are devices that distribute the aroma of essential oils around a room, filling it with fragrance. There are some beautiful diffusers around that are specifically designed to disperse a fine mist of essential oils mixed with water, and are a great addition to any home.

Aromatherapy Massage

An aromatherapy massage is a great way to utilise the benefits of the oils. Using a lotion or oil that usually contains a blend of essential oils, an aromatherapy massage brings relaxation while allowing you to inhale these wonderful aromas as you absorb them into your skin.

Bathing

Many deodorant, bath and shower as well as hair products contain essential oils. Read the label and choose a product that contains pure essential oil. Alternatively add a few drops of concentrated essential oil to your usual, unscented bath, shower and hair products.

Inhalation

Put a few drops of your favourite oil on a tissue and inhale for immediate benefits.

Balancing Chakras

Essential oils have been used for centuries to clear negative energy blockages in the chakras. Specific oils have become associated with the balance of each chakra.

- The crown chakra (Sahasrara) at the top of the head governs the pineal gland and the "inner wisdom" or "higher self". Frankincense, rose, jasmine and lavender correspond with this chakra
- The brow or third eye chakra (Ajna) is located in between the brows connects to the pituitary gland and rules "intuition, memory and mind". Myrrh, sandalwood and jasmine can be used to treat any blockages here
- The throat chakra (Vishuddha) connects to the thyroid gland and relates to "how we communicate". Use lavender, chamomile, clary sage, peppermint and geranium to treat problems arising from this chakra
- The heart chakra (Anahata) affects "love, well-being and compassion", rose, bergamot, chamomile, neroli, sandalwood and palmarosa are its oils
- The solar plexus chakra (Manipura) in the upper abdomen connected to the adrenals and pancreas and is connected to "anxiety, our inner critic and self-esteem". Use ginger, coriander, lavender, marjoram and orange

- The sacral chakra (Svadhisthana) located in the lower abdomen, is linked to the reproductive system and our "sexual presence" and needs sandalwood, ylang ylang, rose, orange or geranium
- The base chakra (Muladhara) at the base of the spine connects us to our ability to feel grounded and safe. Use myrrh, cedarwood, patchouli and vetiver

Put some of your favourite oil in a diffuser and enjoy the Chakra Meditation at www.gaildonnan.com/meditations

Charlotte's Story

When I found Gail, I was at a bit of a cross roads in my life. I was in a job that I was very unhappy in, and I had recently lost my father. I had dreamt of becoming a holistic therapist for years so now was the time! I was searching the internet looking for a massage course when I found The Mindfulspace Wellbeing Company.

I really didn't want to learn in a normal classroom with desks and a blackboard. I wanted to feel what I was learning and that meant the environment had to be right. As soon as I walked into Gail's studio I instantly knew it was for me. Gail put me at ease straight away and we talked for ages. I signed up for the massage course there and then!

I loved every minute of it. I soon found myself signing up for the Indian head massage, meditation and the baby massage instructor courses! Within a few months my dream came true and I became a self-employed holistic therapist. I am now just over a year into having my own business and I'm enjoying life! Gail has become not only my mentor but a good friend and I really value any time that we get to spend together.

The Serene Buddha, Northallerton

"Nature does not hurry, yet everything is accomplished"

Lao Tzu

FINAL THOUGHTS

Chapter 16
Forging Your Path to Well-Being

To enjoy life to the full our physical, mental, spiritual and emotional parts need to be balanced and nurtured.

For our bodies this can be achieved with exercise, good quality sleep, eating well and limiting stimulants.

Taking a break, respecting ourselves, self honouring, spending meaningful time with loved ones and friends together with having a job you love all feed our emotional needs and help generate feelings of belonging.

A sense of purpose together with creativity and time in nature accompanied by an understanding of our energy with regular meditation and mindfulness can help develop our inner wisdom and spirituality.

I hope you have enjoyed working through The Gateway Journey and that you are starting to apply the knowledge and ideas to your own life.

I speak to a lot of people suffering from stress, anxiety and depression which often leaves them feeling like a failure, ineffectual or unproductive. Having personal and professional experience of how the broader implications of stress and anxiety not only can take hold of us but also be managed, I wanted to write this book in order to reach out to you. To demonstrate that it is ok to be frightened of the side effects that stress and anxiety bring, and more importantly how to reduce and remove that fear.

Our state of well-being is not defined by how we earn our money, what we possess, where we live or the car we drive, it comes entirely from within. I hope The Gateway Journey has allowed you to examine your perspective and realise that most of us are already successful and making a huge difference to the world simply by being here.

The inspirational personal stories all point towards the possibility of change being effective through the techniques I have shared and will help you discover a happier and more resilient life.

Making this transition and integrating the techniques explored in The Gateway Journey into everyday life takes time. Introduce small ways to self honour, change your relationship with time, re-read as needed and practice the online meditations and exercises to build up your resilience to stress. Use the breathing exercises, learn how to manage your own energy and recommend or gift this book to a friend.

I would love to continue to support you in your transition so why not sign up for my regular emails, book a place on a Gateway workshop or connect to your inner self with a Gateway retreat; just visit www.gaildonnan.com

"The meaning of life is to find your gift. The purpose of life is to give it away"

Pablo Picasso

Retreat Testimonials

"IT WAS AMAZING!!!!! What an experience. I have taken away more than I could have possibly imagined and found answers to questions I didn't think I had. I was nervous and a little stressed by the time I arrived but I seriously shouldn't have worried. Once the ice was broken and we started to get to know each other the whole weekend flowed beautifully (which is a testament to your organisational skills and skill set). I am struggling to find anything I feel could have been improved upon as I simply had the most amazing experience. "

J M Ripon

"I had a fantastic time thank you. The company was amazing, the location was excellent and all the activities and treatments were great. I do feel that the weekend is excellent value as I got so much out of it and it had plenty of activities and the balance was just right. The one thing that had the most impact on me was the gong sound bath. I feel privileged to have been able to participate in everything and the massage was excellent. All activities were brilliant. My sister would love to book as I would for the next one."

D C Cumbria

"I really enjoyed my time at Trenhouse. I can't ever remember feeling so relaxed and chilled out! Massage, gong bath and meditation, especially the laid down meditation where I felt I could really, really relax. Well done to you and all of the team on a great weekend away. Everything about it was just lovely."

G E Ripon

Further reading

The Power of Now - Eckhart Tolle - New World Library 2004

You Can Heal your Life - Louise Hay - Hay House 1984

Mindfulness Pure & Simple - Oli Doyle - Orion 2014

Notes on a nervous planet - Matt Haigh - Canongate 2018

The Timekeeper - Mitch Albom - Hachette - 2015

The Subtle Art of Not Giving a F*ck - Mark Manson - Harper Collins 2016

Essential Help for Your Nerves - Dr. Claire Weekes 2000

Ikigai - Hector Garcia and Francesc Miralles - Penguin 2017

The Monk Who Sold his Ferrari - Robin Sharma - Harper Collins 1996

Buddhism Plain & Simple - Steve Hagen - Penguin 1997

Buddhism is Not What You Think - Steve Hagen - Penguin 2003

Further listening

Jason Stephenson - www.jasonstephenson.net YouTube & Spotify

The Meditation Podcast - www.themeditationpodcast.com

Insight Timer - www.insighttimer.com

Acknowledgments

I will be eternally grateful to all the people who took the time to contribute their own personal stories for the book, for the students who were happy to write about their journeys and the friends and family who supported the idea in the first place. Particular thanks to Linda More who was my editor and guided me how to put the book together. Thanks to Mark, Alison and Matthew at Colour It In Ltd. Thank you to my husband Craig who is the brightest shining light and to my daughter Evie who is a true inspiration.

Citations

Essential Help for your Nerves - Dr. Claire Weekes - Harper Collins 2000
The Timekeeper - Mitch Albom - Hachette 2015

Other things that helped me get through writing this book

Better You Turmeric Spray
Yogi Bedtime Tea
Bach Flower Rescue Remedy
Neal's Yard Remedies

Namaste

"I Bow To You - the light in me
honours the light in you"
Anon

Gail

These pages are for your own notes

Perhaps identify interesting points from the book or note down any advice that you have found helpful that you can use as an anchor. Make a list of what you want to change with steps on how to ensure it, journal your progress and copy any inspirational quotes to have to hand on your journey.